THE ART OF CHRISTIAN DOUBT

The Art of Christian Doubt

by

J.

FRED DENBEAUX

A HADDAM HOUSE BOOK

Association Press • New York

THE ART OF CHRISTIAN DOUBT

Copyright © 1960 by
National Board of Young Men's Christian Associations

Association Press, 291 Broadway, New York 7, N. Y.

Library of Congress catalog card number: 60-6557

 2

Printed in the United States of America

For my Dulcinea

Preface

THE MODERN MAN IS NOT SO SAFELY REMOVED from primitivism as he may imagine. Or, if he is removed, he may be isolated from reality by doctrines which obscure rather than invite.

Man in the modern age may be prepared to risk everything on a penetration of the physical universe. He may be considerably less willing to risk the penetration of his own mind and psyche.

These essays, deliberately aphoristic and evocative, are intended to involve the reader in those risks which were undertaken by the creative thinkers who laid the foundations for modern civilization.

The essays are dependent upon the reader's willingness

to become involved in the thrusts of the classical world, the world at the foundation of European culture. Unlike most theological treatises they do not depreciate the classical world. Unlike most secular essays they do not ignore the contributions of the Christian faith. The presuppositions of the essays are anchored in the notion that both the classical and the Christian world have made possible man's spiritual flexibility and his intellectual resourcefulness. As such they may be somewhat irritating to both Christians and secularists. However, for those who have taken seriously the contributions of both the church and the university, they may offer some provocative insights.

The writing is intended to involve the reader in debate rather than to provide him with an answer to the problem of existence and purpose. Although the essay is evocative, it does attempt to evoke within the context of history. Therefore, some attempt is made to explicate not only the thrusts of Socrates, the Bible, Christian and humanistic culture but also the retreats of those who found this venture too burdensome.

Contents

Chapter		Page
	Preface	*vii*
1	*The Idea of a Universe*	*1*
	Church and University 6	
	The Examined Life 17	
	The Kingdom of God 20	
	A Double Venture 25	
	Toward Criticism 29	
2	*From Primitivism to Polarization*	*32*
	Pre-Nihilism 34	
	Modern Pyrrhonism 38	
	Contributions of Positivism 44	
	The Limitations of Positivism 47	
	Orthodoxy 51	
	Contemporary Orthodoxy 54	
	The Contributions and Limitations of Orthodoxy 60	
	Polarization 64	

3   *Critical Christianity*   67
        The Old Testament 69
        The New Testament 83

4   *Christian Cultures*   106
        Medieval Religion 113
        Anselm of Canterbury 116
        The Flowering of the Middle Ages 119
        The Modern World 127

5   *Faith and Criticism*   143
        Contemporaneity 146
        Ambiguity 148
        Particularity 163
        Conclusion 168

1 | The Idea of a Universe

RELIGION, LIKE EVERY OTHER CREATIVE IDEA, lives only if it has the daring to spend itself. If it refuses to risk communication, if it wills to protect and preserve itself, it becomes defensive and the slave of its own security system.

Before religion ventures into battle, it must leave its protected battlements. Like a brave knight it must go forth from the safety of the castle. Before it attacks, it must burn its drawbridge. Until the escape route is cut off, religion can risk neither life nor death.

An analysis of Christianity's stake in skepticism must,

[1]

therefore, concern itself with theology's contribution to the art of critical thinking. It cannot concern itself with a defense of Christianity. Nor can it engage in apologetics, the art of explaining the internal validity of the Christian faith. It can only attempt to show that both in its theological center and in its history, Christianity has consistently attempted to demonstrate the meaning of its faith in the context of a critical attitude toward both knowledge and the instruments of that knowledge.

The Christian faith is, in this respect, by no means unique. It cannot claim to have originated the skeptical traditions.[1] It has merely, when it has not retreated into obscurantism, supplemented and, perhaps, added depth to the critical enterprise.

It would be slightly grotesque if a book in defense of skepticism should provide an answer which would eliminate the problem of skepticism. These essays, therefore, are written not to answer a problem but to sustain one. Their stress will be not on the triumph of thought but upon its fragility. Simultaneously an attempt will be made to illuminate not the power but the helplessness of faith. These essays are written for those who believe that intellectual

---

[1] The writer is aware of the fact that this paragraph may sound slightly absurd to the reader. The reader is asked from henceforth to be gracious and, perhaps, see that the author includes the absurd as a method of communication because such a category is, perhaps, the highest form of self-criticism. The absurd is thus an even higher form of indirect communication than is the concept of irony.

creativity emerges out of a marriage between thought and risk, a union between discipline and audacity.

Truth—and with less the sensitive thinker can never be concerned—never appears as a finished product. Just as answers can never really be separated from questions, so, too, can truth never be divorced from the ground out of which it grew. Truth which is separated from the question becomes something less than truth, an abstraction . . . a lifeless doctrine.

Man is a most problematic being. What he is by definition and what he is in fact are separated by infinity. Both law and custom define man as having both rights and responsibilities apart from the other animals. But the legal definition only protects rights: it cannot confer reality. Beyond definition there is an Olympian mountain that man must climb if he is to become truly human.

Rather than to risk the mountain he sometimes prefers to throw himself over the first crevasse. Terrified by the demands of being truly civilized, he may slide into . . . skid row. Rather than risk everything on the Everest of becoming human, he may, rather, choose to live in the village below sharpening pitons, mending rope, and growing rich supplying tools to those who gamble everything on the mountain. And so, both the man on skid row and the bourgeois man are protected from becoming human. To become human in fact, and not by mere definition, is a very dangerous art, indeed.

Once there was one who saw that God's glory could saturate the earth only if man abandoned himself in utter innocency:

> "Let the children come to me, and do not
> hinder them: for to such belongs the
> kingdom of God. Truly, I say to you,
> whoever does not receive the kingdom of
> God like a child shall not enter it."[2]

To become really human under such an invitation is so exciting and so dangerous that before its possibility the heart must tremble. It is easier to count money or get drunk than to risk everything on the hungry flames that burn and sear until the universe be glorified.

But if a man does not want to see the universe come afire, he can find ways and means of avoiding the spark. There are, of course, many ways of polarizing life. One of the most obvious is either to dismiss the dreams and visions which have excited the imagination, or to dismiss the fact that these visions have had little or no demonstration.

Man, uninformed by the visions of the community, untutored by its symbols, knows only chaos. As a sheerly biological individual he knows only the chaos of sense impressions. He becomes human in a sense that the community through parents, schools, and church communicates to him the forms which organize sense experience into meaningful patterns.

---

[2] Luke 18:16, 17.

The community teaches him that there is a moral order, that justice is a valid concept, that a universe truly exists. But he is frustrated because his sense experience teaches him that he has never seen the abstractions of beauty, truth, and goodness about which the community speaks.

Which are right, the visions of the community or the stubborn pressures of sense experience? If he chooses to place his trust in the world of sense experience he will be compelled to dismiss the hopes of humanity. If he chooses to believe some combination of these hopes, he may be tempted to dismiss the world of sense experience. In the first case, he may end up as an atheist and an iconoclast; in the second case, he may end up as a naïve and possibly dishonest believer.[3]

And yet it may be the temptation to oversimplify, to drive truth into irreconcilable zones which both gives man his security and dehumanizes him. And here may well be the origin of sin, the acceptance of polarized immaturity rather than creative complexity.

And yet the awareness of sin produces hope. There will be those who will forego the cheap answers of both ortho-

---

[3] The tension between institutional religion and sensitive literature is a tragic one. Thus, the modern man who would like to be religious is always embarrassed to discover that the therapy of the theater is sometimes more powerful than that of the church. The church, of course, promises more but frequently lacks the redemptive catharsis of a Tennessee Williams who in "A Streetcar Named Desire" promises less but produces more.

doxy and dogmatic atheism. They will seek, in the agony of their own integrity, to hold together the most ultimate mystery of life, the profound relationship between problem and truth, between question and answer. These, seeking to live on the abyss, will turn to those who can teach them of the dialogue which reflects the rhythm of the universe.

CHURCH AND UNIVERSITY

There are many communities which do communicate the courage by which men are enabled to believe that the universe has order and rhythm. Politicians, members of the judiciary, and educators necessarily presuppose a world which is more than "sound and fury signifying nothing."[4]

Political parties, however, are inadequate in sustaining such a vision for two reasons. In the first place, their interpretation of a moral universe is a little shopworn because of its involvement with their obvious self-interest: they are attempting to gain or secure power through the idea of a moral order. Second, the politician who can gain power rarely possesses the quality of imagination which can enable him to escape platitudes.

---

[4] It is the judiciary in the modern world which is most disappointing as an interpreter of a moral universe. Thus, the heirs of Stoic law and Roman jurisprudence consistently fail to produce jurists who understand that the complex cases which they master are more than accidents, that the case histories, themselves, represent an analogy to the moral pattern of the universe.

The university, however, does reflect something of the order and vitality of that universe which it seeks to serve. Whoever has labored in a university cannot help being impressed with its interior spirit, a microcosm of a gracious and powerful universe, a community which is concerned with . . . truth.

The university, however, is not an autonomous unit. It is, to an extent, dependent upon the creative vitalities of the society of which it is a part. The fact that contemporary American society finds itself in a defensive relation to a power which threatens it both militarily and ideologically taints the freedom of inquiry which should be characteristic of a free society. More and more, especially in the sciences, does the university become an adjunct of the political anxiety of the community. Less and less is it really free.

Second, the university suffers because of its own inability to find an ideology which will give grandeur to the technological society with which it is in rapport. To a large extent, the university is the victim of fragmentation. The achievement of status depends upon specialization and, by the time that status is achieved, it is almost impossible for the thinker to be concerned about so unspecialized a dimension as the universe. But, without the universe as a protagonist, every discipline is threatened with the loss of vitality. The result is that the specialist is not really free to engage in risk thinking. In better than a generation, neither a Platonist nor an Hegelian has had a significant voice in the interpretation of the university's involvement with the universe. A technological world has left its mark upon abstract thought so that more and more, the university mind lives within the presuppositions of empiricism; less and less is it enabled to relate to a world possessing metaphysical pretensions. There is, of course, no reason why there should not be strong empirical tradition, but if empiricism, or any system for that matter, dominates, then the university has lost its richest possession, intellectual diversity. And when the rainbow of the mind gives way to a dull monochrome there is little hope that the university will risk the experience of living on the boundary.

The modern man has hoped for a philosophy which would enable him to see that the chaotic world of his experience was connected to a meaningful universe. Frustrated by the low estate of political thinking, isolated from the rarified disciplines of scholarship, he has, in increasingly large numbers, turned to the church. It is likely that he turned not to escape from political and intellectual life but because, intuitively, he knew that the church had absorbed and attempted to renew the vitalities both of the mind and of political life.

On the one hand, it must be said that the church has fulfilled its role. Regardless of its weaknesses, and they are numberless, the church has represented to the world the idea of a universe which is both disciplined and compassionate. In the course of the historical development of Christianity it has, sometimes reluctantly, accepted the pressures from every symbol of universal insight. Thus it has successively absorbed and transposed Roman and Stoic law, Greek metaphysics, and later more empirical philosophies of existence. The church—and sometimes it has dragged its heels—has provided a home for every idea which has struggled to comprehend the reality of the universe. Even those communions, the strongly Protestant and Reformation churches, which have denied the legitimacy of the Platonic-Aristotelian-Stoic world view have themselves been intellectually sharpened before the extraordinary protagonist with which they have done battle. The church has found that either it must absorb the wisdom of the classical view of the universe or it must live in creative tension with that view. In any case it has never been able to disregard those who considered that experience was grounded in cosmos rather than chaos.

And yet from an opposite point of view religion has been a failure for, while with its left hand it has pointed to the vitality and reality of the universe, with its right hand it has insisted upon burying that vitality in the cemetery of its own rigid doctrines. In part the church has failed because it has refused to take seriously its responsibility for the life of the mind, of law, and of politics. In abstracting itself from life it has gained a dubious security. In doing so it has lost the vitality that goes with risk.

[9]

Thus the church, like the university, has eliminated the problematic dimension of thought and faith. It has cast its weight on the side of answers instead of questions. Seldom has a community been less aware of the precariousness of its own presuppositions, seldom has a community wrestled less with the agony of justifying its own existence. Thus the church has spoken with authority generally only in the area of the trivial.

As the world has become burdened by greater complexity the church has retreated into simplicity. It faces a world which has been terrified by hunger, revolution, and nuclear war. But the church instead of living on the boundary of its own guilt merely retreats into the moral principles of the nineteenth century.[5] Thus the church, enervated by the examples of both communism and the memories of McCarthyism, takes few chances. As a result it speaks with little creative wisdom.[6] Thus, as we shall see, though ancient

---

[5] The church prefers the simpler ethics of the frontier society to the more complex ethics of a collective and industrialized society. Anchored to that single dogma created by American Christianity, absolute separation of church and state, the church generally prefers to think in terms of individual piety rather than the problems of the welfare state. The fact that the modern world faces difficult and intricate problems does not prevent the church from concentrating on a prairie ethic.

[6] The issues of race, disarmament especially in the field of nuclear weapons, diplomacy are of course related. American political thinking, weakened by the emergence of communism as a world power, has been unable to "risk" new strategies. One thinks for instance of our

theology had involved itself in the creative options of philosophy and art, the modern Protestant church has relieved itself of ambiguity by retreating into a one-dimensional pietism.

As a result of its retreat the church not only has lost critical power but also has jeopardized its sensitivity. Protestantism, whether in South Africa or in Little Rock, has so seriously compromised its moral conscience that it is unlikely to regain its voice for generations. By accepting its sociological situation rather than its prophetic responsibility the church has lost its capacity to measure itself by the magnificent but ruthless justice of the universe.

Because it will not judge itself, it cannot confront the civilization with a witness to that radical gospel which it claims to serve. It proclaims a resurrection unconnected with interior agony.

Christianity, now that Marxism has been eliminated from the American scene, feels itself to be secure.[7] As a result

---

stubborn refusal to grant diplomatic recognition to the Peiping government and our consequent failure to have any relationship with the peoples of a nation which may rapidly be becoming the most powerful nation of the earth. Failure to maintain diplomatic and commercial relationships eliminates the possibility of our assessing, from the *inside,* the growth of a nation which may, if we do not understand the rhythm and interior logic of that growth, in the end, hasten our own destruction.

[7] The church may take small comfort in recognizing that the problem which it faces is one which belongs to the general culture. A generation has grown up without having witnessed an act of self-

it has become gross and torpid because of its apparent triumph over opposition. Having, at least for a season, discredited atheism, the horizons of the church grow narrower and narrower. No wind blows in the airless rooms of ecclesiastical piety. Fed by the rich diet of its triumph the church may yet strangle on its oily virtue.

And the church cannot survive on mere piety. It too is involved in the life of the mind as well as in the art of politics. Indeed the present stage of a truce among the three is like a thieves' agreement. Until church and university face each other critically a genuinely open and exciting intellectual atmosphere cannot emerge. Unless challenging and vigorous debate emerges each will continue to retreat into the forms of obscurantism in which they each feel comfortable. There is, after all, little to choose from between esoteric scholarship and obscurantist piety.

---

criticism on the part of the Republic. A civilization has emerged which has twisted its critical faculties so that they bear only upon alien cultures or upon those who are accused of giving aid and comfort to the enemy. Not for a decade have its moral sinews been tested. Indeed, except for the victories over the great depression of the 30's, over Fascism in the 40's, the nation has, with the exception of the Korean War, known only confusion compounded by leadership without originality and diplomacy without daring. The generation now growing to maturity has been stimulated only by the gospel of a balanced budget. Without hope it cannot sit in judgment upon itself. Hopeless, it can only surrender to security. Worshiping security, it cannot think critically or imagine creatively. All that it can do is to react nervously and compulsively against any complex of powers which would dislodge it from . . . its security.

But what if the need for criticism has been forgotten? What if the culture as a whole has forgotten that there is a truth, a truth so holy that man must stand before it in utter humility?

If the very idea of truth has been forgotten, then man cannot be surprised that passion and power have vanished from the universe. Perhaps the greatness of the modern man is that he remembers that once there was a flame where now only gray ashes exist.

But there can never be a fresh flame so long as men pretend that gray ashes are sufficient. New power will come only if man cleans out his dead hearth and, as men have done before him, builds a fresh and vigorous fire.

But even as men try to build a fresh structure of burning ideas, they will face two terrifying obstacles. Intrigued by their own heroism, they may tempt themselves to believe that they are their own creators. Contemptuously dismissing the authority and the forms of the past they may insist that the universe conform only to their own fresh organization. Excited by the novelty of their ideas and composition, they may well be innocent of the fact that the fires which they have builded have been lit before. However, not many will be diverted by this temptation, because there are limited numbers of heroic and creative people.

The most dangerous temptation, by far, will come to those multitudes of well-meaning people who will think that light and truth are gained through an identification with the past. Both clergymen and teachers, for instance, attempt to invest the past with an authority which is designed to shape the present. However, in serving the past so naïvely, they may distort its design. There are, thus, any number of clergymen and theologians who identify themselves with certain propositions about Jesus, but who, perhaps, fail to understand that Jesus lived dangerously in a world unsupported by self-evident propositions. In the same manner, there are many historians of philosophy with organized systems of almost invulnerable information about Socrates but who have not, perhaps, understood why it was that Socrates walked on the precarious tightropes of thought rather than sat on heavy packages of information. Thus, the servants of the past, both clergy and professors, tend to organize the past in such a way that they are, themselves, freed from the existential anguish which initially shaped the creativity of the past. It is because the training of youth is in the hands, not of the hero but of the professor and the clergyman, that we have to fear not the emergence of dangerous fires but, rather, the development of a gallery of photographs of fires that are long since dead. And, it is precisely this kind of deadly organization of the past which may keep youth from ever having a present.

And yet, the very heroes who make up the past themselves, discovered a creative and exciting universe because they dared to live in their present. Therefore, children are taught to identify themselves with ancient heroics. But to remember that once men leaped is not the same as leaping for oneself. It is not enough to be taught that once a heroic stride was taken. Even if the names of such pioneers are engraved on the memories of children, they, themselves, will not become human until they leap beyond those who have gone before. It is always possible to teach children to imitate, to go through the motions of spirited thinking. So a child may learn to pump a tune out of the piano by hitting keys which follow the numbers on a colored chart. The tune will come, but it will not be music; for music, like every art of civilization, is an exercise of freedom.

Perhaps leaping is feared because freedom is dreaded. Thus, it is safer to teach men to remember than to adventure. And so, conservatives, both of the church and of the university, make it their task to consolidate and to classify the leaps that resolute men once took. Civilization ceases to be a challenging art and becomes a heavy monument. Civilization, like an obsolete destroyer, is preserved in a gray plastic blanket.

And yet, though a mechanical reliance on the past can obscure it, it can also represent a daring introduction to the present. It is precisely because man has a past that he is free. Possessing a history man knows that he exists apart from nature.

The modern man has developed many new sources of energy, but the possibility of free existence he did not create. The possibility of that freedom comes from the past, from the knowledge of those who first moved from primitivism into some confidence in the reliability of the universe.

And civilization, the sense that past and present are purposefully and aesthetically related, came into being in the ancient Mediterranean world because some dared to assume that underlying the chaos of life there was a cosmos.

The student of history may never fully comprehend the mystery by which the Mediterranean man, whether Mycenaean, Hellenic, or Judean, developed the faith by which he could accept a meaningful universe. Yet, it was the venture of that man which has ever since enabled successive generations to understand that they, too, *must* leap; and, leaping, they have left the enduring signs of their spiritual arabesques in architecture, music, and philosophy.

Such a union of thought and imagination later man may never take for granted. Such a venture is analogous to the art of the high-wire walker. The art is exhilarating and, if the nerve of courage fail, suicidal.

The universe, the sense for a world of purpose and meaning, does not exist in the flats of life. The universe is ventured or it is not gained. Those who are prepared to penetrate the past, instead of merely classifying it, *will* be given the courage to have a present. And, although the ancients can never be imitated, it is reassuring to know that there were some who did not retreat but who leaped across the crevasse.

THE EXAMINED LIFE

The idea of an intelligible world, the notion that there existed a truth to which man could be related and fulfilled, flowered neither in the forest nor in the swamp. It came into being under the impact of the city states of the ancient world. In Athens, Jerusalem, and Rome men chose to consider a basis for their actions other than mere tradition. Out of the deliberations of countless marketplaces a series of related ideas began to emerge which communicated the faith that experience, so apparently chaotic and conflicting, had a unifying ground: that man was confronted by an intelligent and intelligible universe.

The originality of this assumption, the faith that a dynamic universe does exist, has lost its grandeur only because the contemporary world has taken the idea for granted. The image of primitive man venturing forth from his cave, daring to break out of his intellectual jungle, is nothing short of magnificent.

The idea of civilization as a mirror to the ultimate order and love of the universe came into being, in the main, because of the affirmations of two classical cultures, the Graeco-Roman and the Hebraic. These two cultures can best be understood by examining the two historical figures who best illustrated the scope and daring of the traditions which they represented and transformed. Indeed, the grandeur and power of European civilization is understandable only as a refinement and continuous reinterpretation of the minds of Socrates of Athens and Jesus of Nazareth.

Since the Greek period there have been many philosophers who developed analytical systems that were far more complex than that of Socrates, but no one since has surpassed this pioneer in intellectual courage. Socrates will always be remembered as the thinker who first dramatized the fact that the order of the human mind was linked to the order of the universe. He brought stability to conceptualization by showing that for those who possessed the courage, eternity could be found at the end of an idea.

It was Socrates who illustrated the fact that truth was to be found only by means of the ordered mind of . . . each human being. Truth arises only out of the intellect's activity and can never be found in uncritical assumptions, dogmas, or authorities. Neither a general nor an emperor is vested with more truth than is given to a trained mind. Only the mind can determine that there is a stable reality at the ground of all knowledge.[8] When the intellect gains the courage to emancipate itself from the senses, when she follows out the logic of her own structure, then she may know, not the shadowy world of appearances, but true being.[9] By following the logic of her courage, the mind is forced to conclude that the basis of knowledge comes not

---

8 Phaedrus 247.

9 Phaedo 65.

from the accumulation of sense data, but from an awareness which it possessed before she began to move in that floundering sensual world. The mind, therefore, it may be concluded, possessed the knowledge of the true, the good, and the beautiful before it was born. Therefore, it must be assumed that the mind or soul, since its knowledge cannot be proved on any other grounds, is immortal and not affected, except through wrong choice, by the world of sense.[10]

Each man possesses this knowledge within his structure as a human being. No teacher can give it to him, for the teacher is merely a midwife who helps him to trust the eternal world with which his mind is connected. Each mind, therefore, once it takes its courage in hand, can move out of the world of the shadows and, by clear thinking, dwell in knowledge of eternal truth.

As a result of the magic of this kind of thinking, the immediate followers of Socrates, Plato, and Aristotle were able to communicate a somewhat more complicated analysis of the nature of being and the instruments by which man appraises it. As such, in the Socratic, Platonic, Aristotelian continuum, Western man has received a library of writings which has helped to liberate him from error. Stimulated by Socratic courage, he has developed the intellectual tools which have enabled him to move increasingly from the original quicksand of primitivism to a degree of mastery

---

[10] Phaedo 76.

over nature. As man acquired the courage to think, he also acquired the faith to trust his world. Saved from darkness and a demon infested natural world, man gained a sense of his transcendency over nature. Trusting the order of the world, his own mind developed so that he became an analyzing human being instead of merely being the passive recipient of nature's terrors. Power was transferred from the outer darkness to the interior mind of man.

THE KINGDOM OF GOD

To understand the foundations of Western civilization it is necessary to see the degree with which Western man has bound together both the criticism and the creativity of Jesus of Nazareth and Socrates of Athens.

Jesus, like Socrates, gives a classical form to the murky and sprawling traditions which preceded him. He too faces an age which cannot escape cynicism and superstition. Like Socrates, Jesus affirms a new vision of truth and, like Socrates, for this affirmation he dies.

Jesus the Jew, unlike Socrates the Greek, found the rhythms of eternity in history and not in nature. Just as Socrates represented a tradition which could not identify reality with the immediate, with a sense experience, so Jesus represented a tradition which could not identify reality with political power. Thus the prophetic mind insisted on a radical break with political idolatry just as the Greeks insisted on a complete break with magic or the idolatry of nature.

Both the prophets and Jesus refused to accept the finality of emperors. Inherently skeptical of concentrations of power the prophets could cry:

> Woe to those who go down to
>   Egypt for help
> And rely on horses,
> Who trust in chariots because they
>   are many
> And in horsemen because they are
>   very strong.[11]

Nor did this criticism of a foreign power mean an uncritical attitude toward national power. Thus from the earliest days of the monarchy the critical prophets could remind, nay inform, the kings that they had violated a law which was their task to serve.[12]

Jesus, the child of a prophetic culture, was necessarily skeptical of the entrenched idolatries of history. However, and again like both Socrates and the prophets, the critical dimensions of the mind of Jesus did not end in nihilism. Skepticism did not become an end in itself but rather was dialectically linked with faith itself. The skeptical method

---

[11] Isaiah 31:1.

[12] In contrast with the usual identification of Eastern rulers with divinity the kings of Israel had a hard time. Thus Nathan announced that David was a thief, Elijah attacked Ahab because he had appropriated land that belonged to a citizen, and Amos announced that one of Israel's mightiest kings would, because of his insensitivity to the problems of power, *die by the sword.*

became an instrument by which Jesus hazarded a purer truth. Just as Socrates moved from the confusions of sense to the clarities of the mind, so Jesus moved from a critical denial of the sufficiency of human power to the assumption of a pure and cosmic power. It is in this creativity, grounded in a prophetic and critical method, that Jesus makes his most exciting and enduring contribution.

The creative faith of Jesus was expressed in the notion that although an ultimate order could not be identified with any temporal power, nevertheless *the kingdom of God is at hand.* Thus, if Jesus had lived in the realm of logic instead of poetry, his interpretation of life could have been expressed in the idea that existence is the dimension in which God and man meet. Or, to put it in another way, the creative faith of Jesus insisted that a universal and just order was linked to the life of man.

Man lives truly when he believes that his existence is with God. Man lives sinfully when he will not and dares not believe that God is nigh. In the great epics of Israel the dramatic tension is between those who cannot believe that God is underwriting history and those who believe that human existence is connected to the life of God.[13] Thus the

---

[13] References to the words *linked* and *connected* are not to indicate either that man is an extension of God or that he is grimly and self-effacingly under God. The biblical faith is one neither of pantheism nor of synthetic self-abasement. Rather man is asked to believe that he lives truly and magnificently if his life is with God, and that he evaporates or sins if he departs from living with God.

problem of Israel is that it must always believe that its own existence is not independent and that at the same time its existence, even if that existence be dressed in a tattered despair, is meaningful because it is shared by God. Thus, as Israel flees from slavery and security into the terrors of the wilderness, it is asked to believe that

> . . . the Lord went before them by day
> In a pillar of cloud to lead them
>   along the way,
> And by night in a pillar of fire to
>   give them light,
> That they might travel by day and by
>   night;
> The pillar of cloud by day and the
>   pillar of fire by night did not
>   depart from before the people.[14]

The problem of Israel, however, is that it cannot believe that God is so linked.

> When Pharaoh drew near, the people of Israel
>   lifted up their eyes, and behold, the
>   Egyptians were marching after them;
> And they were in great fear.
> And the people of Israel cried out to
>   the Lord; and they said to Moses,
> "Is it because there are no graves in

---

[14] Exodus 13:21-22.

Egypt that you have taken us away to
die in the wilderness?
What have you done to us, in bringing
us out of Egypt?
Is not this what we said to you in Egypt,
'Let us alone and let us serve the Egyptians'?
For it would have been better for us to
serve the Egyptians than to die in the
wilderness."[15]

But Jesus believed that God was nigh. He proclaimed
that a world was about to emerge in which goodness would
reign. A world was a-borning in which all who have need
would be satisfied. The reader of the Gospels has the impression that God cannot be held off, that He invades human history, that He demands his share of existence. When
He comes the hungry will be fed, the lonely will be ad-
dressed, the naked will be clothed, prisoners will be vis-
ited, and sinners will be forgiven. God's benevolent power
will heal the scars which man has suffered because of his
own abuse of power.

The followers of Jesus take his message so seriously that
they not only believe that history can be and is being redeemed from its tragedies but that it is redeemed by a
God who does not hold himself apart, who heals by bear-
ing the suffering of man. Thus, the passage which best epi-

---

[15] Exodus 14:10-12.

tomizes the biblical conception of the divine-human mu-
tuality speaks of a God who, sharing human tears, renews
existence.

> And I heard a great voice from the
>   throne saying,
> "Behold, the dwelling of God is with men.
> He will dwell with them, and they shall
>   be his people,
> And God himself will be with them;
> He will wipe away every tear from
>   their eyes,
> And death shall be no more. . . .[16]

Like Socrates Jesus formalizes a critical and a creative
faith which enables his followers to believe that existence
is sacred and not expendable. For those who have been influenced by Jesus there must always be the sense that the
kingdom of God is at hand.

A DOUBLE VENTURE

The art of civilization has not been achieved primarily because of man's technical triumph over nature. It has been
achieved because Western man has been willing to be
stimulated by the traditions of Jesus and Socrates. Each
communicated the notion that man could be fulfilled only
by denying an apparent truth and by serving a more ulti-

---

[16] Revelation 21:3-4.

mate truth. Both held that neither tradition, nor clan, nor family, nor the requirements of the state could be placed above man's obligation to the true kingdom.[17]

The credo of Socrates was that the *unexamined life is not worth living*.[18] This assumption, that rational examination would relate every man who undertook its risks to a universal truth, ruined the idea that truth was a matter of opinion. The cosmos is not a tumbledown shack in which slovenly minds may dwell. Not so; the universe has been more carefully engineered than that. The universe is a home for those who will tune their minds to its iron demands. Truth exists independently of erroneous opinions no matter how tenaciously they are defended.

Socrates' judges, those who condemned him to die, could

---

[17] I would not want to irritate either classical or biblical scholars by suggesting that Jesus and Socrates were identical. Indeed they are not! Frequently they have been placed in unnecessary conflict by their defenders. Yet each represented a great richness as well as a limitation. Jesus, because of his own traditions, had not been made sufficiently sensitive to the Socratic problem, the problem of ignorance and superstition. In discovering the rhythms of nature and the human mind, the biblical world is weak. When civilized man seeks to overcome his own superstitions, he does better to turn to Socrates. At the same time the mind of Jesus provides greater help if the civilized man is attempting to overcome his idolatries, including the idolatry of the mind itself. Nevertheless one would have to say that ultimately the mind of Jesus and the mind of Socrates are neither in ultimate conflict nor in identity, but are, out of their respective cultures, analogically related to each other.

[18] *Apology*, p. 38.

not see that he had communicated a conviction which was to make every man into an Odysseus of the intellect, in pursuit of a truth which was sacred and attainable. Socrates forged an instrument by which every man could joyfully and vigorously chasten every primitive limitation. With such a conviction truth emerged, not as the tool of parochial interests, but as the link with the eternal world. It was unconquerable and unshakable. It became the Magna Charta of human experience as it broke down the distinction between the learned and the unlearned, the rich and the poor, and gave to each man the exhilarating obligation of thinking . . . in tune with a universe which was a mirror to his own intellectual discipline.

Similarly Jesus combined criticism with creativity. By pointing up the distinction between Caesar's order and God's order he depreciated the idolatries usually communicated through political loyalties and at the same time avoided a meaningless relativism. The followers of Jesus were placed in the position of being necessarily critical of existing power and at the same time committed to the restitution of a higher righteousness.

The church has, since, frequently escaped its difficult task of criticizing political injustice while simultaneously stimulating new patterns of justice. Refusing to become an extension of Caesar's realm it frequently abjures political involvement. At the same time, that same church has left behind a body of theory which testifies to its faith that the

Messiah is involved with the world of power. Thus, both Catholicism and the Reformed faith have—either through doctrines of natural law or through providence—acknowledged that man can make relevant political decisions precisely because God cannot be isolated from man's organization of his existence.

Indeed, it is the involvement of God with common life that provides the Christian with both his detachment and his hope. Because God is not identical with normal process, the Christian has critical powers that are denied to both the bourgeois and the Marxist man. Because God is not isolated from the problems of power the Christian is forced to believe in the redemption of the community.

Jesus focuses man's mind upon both dimensions. As the Immanuel of God he reminds history that God is linked to human affairs. God's life and man's life are not identical, but neither are they separable. Immanuel, or *God with us,* means that the ultimate is bonded to the ordinary, the sacred is wedded to the profane. The acceptance of that bond involves an act far more demanding of both mind and spirit than does either the identification of God with experience or the banishment of God to nonexistence.

✳   ✳   ✳

It will have occurred to some readers that the analysis so far has failed to answer the question as to the truth or falsity of the double visions communicated through the Socratic and Christian traditions. The omission is deliberate. It is impossible, standing in safety, to measure that reality which lies beyond the frontiers which Jesus and Socrates crossed. No IBM machine, no microscope, no set of statistics can determine the validity of the visions that they communicated. Certainly this cannot be achieved in an essay on skepticism. However, it is possible to discuss Jesus and Socrates even if they cannot be measured. Both made an historical contribution which pressed the emerging civilization to the point where it had to act critically toward both opinion and power.

TOWARD CRITICISM

What contribution have the visions of Socrates and Jesus made toward intellectual criticism and sensitivity of spirit? It may seem to the reader that the creation of a vision of the universe has the opposite effect, namely that it eliminates the possibility of disengaged thinking. Only at first glance is this true. Skepticism, it will be remembered, does not exist within primitivism. There, man is the prey of endless fears and unconquered anxieties. He lacks the instruments to transcend an environment filled with chaos and demonic forces. The skeptical principles of Jesus and Socrates were directed against the assumption that experience was limited to chaos. Creating a new assumption, that an orderly universe existed, they used this principle to criticize arbitrariness in the areas of opinion and injustice.

If Socrates and Jesus were right a new conception of the critical life emerges. Faith ceases to be viewed as an exercise disengaged from reality. Skepticism ceases to be understood in a purely negative role. Instead, faith and skepticism are viewed as the expression of man's two most basic needs. United, although frequently reluctantly, faith and skepticism become the two foci of the critical method.[19]

According to this method faith acquires discipline; and skepticism, responsibility. The linkage within such a critical method creates a new kind of mind, one which enables man to maneuver both negatively and positively instead of being lost in the nondialectical latitudes of an empty faith and an even emptier doubt.

The development of European civilization has thus mirrored a movement which is at the ground of all experience. The rhythm of the universe is always both critical and creative. The fact that the Greeks were first compelled to say *no* to sense enabled them to gain some understanding of the

---

[19] Western thought has, to be sure, other conceptions of skepticism. One thinks of doubt used as a methodological tool in Descartes. Skepticism has, in formal philosophy, also simply represented rational man's refusal to adjust his intellectual antenna to any mystery which arises beyond his own competence. Although these views are the most prevalent they seem lacking in seriousness. Descartes, as Pascal saw, was a little too contrived. Absolute skepticism on the other hand, ends in nihilism. One could find better illustrations of doubt by turning from philosophy to literature. A Hamlet and a Raskolnikov plumb the depths of doubt which the surface exercise of the rationalist cannot duplicate.

universality of being. The fact that the Hebrews found it necessary first to say *no* to kings enabled them to discover a justice which was both divine and universal.

The dialectical method of criticism and creativity, of doubt and faith, of question and answer, created the possibility of civilization. Through this method man has escaped the tyranny both of nature and of dictators. Skeptical of any easy identification of reality with the immediate and the superficial, man has been thrust into ever wider circles of knowledge. Through criticism he has conquered his parochialism; through his creativity he has found a universe.

2 | *From Primitivism to Polarization*

AN OBSERVER OF MAN'S CULTURAL DEVELOP-
ment might heave a sigh of relief once he had moved from
the prison of primitivism to the freedom of living in a com-
prehensible universe. The idea of the universe, whether in
the form expressed by Socrates or Jesus, not only demanded
a response but assured man that his response, whether in
love or in thinking, was related to the nature of the universe itself.

Man has succeeded through his art, political theory, and
philosophical speculation in communicating the idea of the
cosmos expressed by an Athenian thinker and a Jewish mes-

siah. The Cathedral of Chartres reveals that the logic of the universe is written into its stones. The law code of Justinian and the charter of the United Nations reflect the Christian-Stoic conviction that a moral universe exists. One has only to read portions of the *Summa Theologica* to see, whether one agrees with St. Thomas' premises or not, that the mind of man is wondrously and intricately wrought. Western civilization therefore represents man's continuing dialogue with the idea of the universe as he tries passionately to reshape that idea to fit new experiences.

An observer watching man would soon discover, however, that the victory over primitivism is never either automatic or permanent. The disciplines of Jesus and Socrates can either become a springboard to freedom or lead to a new prison. In the hands of their disciples those disciplines have become both.

Man is not free because he takes a single step. He must continue to walk in freedom. A chain-gang lockstep, though giving the appearance of motion, is not free. Simulated freedom, an intellectual lockstep, has taken two forms which have plagued man ever since he began to take the universe seriously.

The first form can be defined as Pyrrhonism, the second as orthodoxy. These positions stand at opposite poles. Frequently they feed on each other's mistakes and allow the truth to fall in the middle. Pyrrhonism, named after Pyrrho, a fourth century B.C. critic of the Socratic view of an orderly cosmos, is a form of skepticism which holds that knowledge is impossible and which, furthermore, is unconcerned about its impossibility. Orthodoxy, on the other hand, is the position that triumphs in any creative movement, whenever a classic definition emerges. Then man attempts to relate himself to the classic definition rather than to the dynamic realities which called the definition into being. Pyrrhonism is damned sure that the universe does not exist. Orthodoxy is damned certain that it does. Each, having taken its position out of the smelting furnace and allowed the slag to harden, is unwilling to examine the alternative.

PRE-NIHILISM

Perhaps the greatest intellectual achievement of European civilization is buried in the *Summa Theologica*. St. Thomas Aquinas created an almost indestructible synthesis between Aristotle, the philosophical heir of Socrates, and Christianity, the theological heir of Jesus. Through Aquinas the idea of the universe received a double definition.[1] Indeed, even Protestant theologians would agree that if a synthesis between the pagan and the Christian world *were* necessary, the synthesis of St. Thomas would constitute the classical

---

[1] Protestants who tend to be compulsively critical of St. Thomas need to remember that Aquinas can be appreciated even though he is disagreed with. From the point of view of aesthetics, no other thinker has achieved such symmetry in the development of his system.

form. Catholicism, in making the philosophy of St. Thomas official, has obviously given a finality to the form which St. Thomas created.

Unfortunately this synthesis, like every other successful definition, became classical and official; in short, it became orthodox and slowly but surely dried up the streams of reality. Once the definition became authoritative, it lost some of its grandeur. Even worse, the structure froze into fixed position not only the brilliant insights but also the errors of the Aristotelian and Christian methodology. Thus, the repudiation of Aristotle, indeed the repudiation of the whole Christian apparatus of thought, became a necessity if men were to breathe the air of intellectual freedom again. The Renaissance repudiated not only the Aristotelian method but also the entire medieval synthesis itself. The elemental hunger for fresh experience which had not been pre-digested came into being.

> There came an epoch when Christianity—
> possibly wearying of metaphysical ex-
> ploration—looked around and took note
> of the existence of the great world,
> and thereupon discovered new reasons for
> living.[2]

Out of this hunger for life a new interest in the universe

---

[2] Samivel, and Audrain, M.: *The Glory of Egypt* (New York: Vanguard Press, 1955), p. 11.

arose, an interest characterized by the concern for direct communication. In part this directness was reflected in the mysticism of thinkers like Paracelsus and Giordano Bruno. But the primary form of the rebellion against Aquinas and Aristotle did not take the form of an enthusiasm for nature. Rather the decisive attack, as far as the modern world is concerned, on Aristotle-Aquinas consisted of a repudiation of thought based upon inference. Judgments of nature were to be based not on universals but on particulars. Francis Bacon provided the clues which, later, men like John Locke and David Hume developed into the modern scientific method. That method, the enemy of all untested assumptions, provided the basis for modern technological civilization. As it repudiated the world of the universal idea, it ushered in the world of the machine. It substituted a white-coated scientist for a black-robed priest.

Insofar as the scientific method did provide man with a direct method of observing and classifying the measurable rhythms of nature, it made a contribution which cannot be minimized. It enabled man to gain control over the effects of nature in a way which restored to man that mastery which, in medieval thought, had been more theoretical than actual. It gave him the knowledge and the power to attack disease and hunger. He was thus enabled to enrich life to a degree reserved previously for only a fortunate few.

Insofar as the modern scientific method has made a creative contribution it was not Pyrrhonistic. This is to say that although critical of Socrates-Plato-Aristotle, it has not necessarily become the prisoner of its own attack. It has gone forward and created new and stimulating techniques for understanding the cosmos through an appreciation of the detailed laws by which that cosmos seems to be ordered. In the wake of this contribution it has, happily, eliminated a great deal of superstition and nonsense about the universe. Socrates may have conceived of an orderly universe, but it was the modern scientist who developed a method by which that insight could be tested and supported.

If the greatest intellectual achievement of medieval Europe was the *Summa Theologica,* then the greatest intellectual achievement of the modern world has been the conquest of nature by an infinite number of laboratory scientists. The victory over Aristotle was obviously not a total loss. And the modern world has witnessed its own pioneers grappling not with the idea of the universe, but with the concrete way in which it seems to tick. Both the thought and the analysis of the rhythm give substance and confidence to all who have believed that man faces not broken shards, but a graceful vessel of experience. However, the failure of the laboratory mind to concern itself with the world of metaphysical and aesthetic imagination has prepared the ground for intellectual nihilism.

MODERN PYRRHONISM

If human creativity depends upon the idea of a universe, the insight that a meaningful reality underlies the seeming fragmentation of experience, then the most nihilistic attack upon that creativity comes from a school of thought called logical positivism.[3] In the sense that logical positivism has eliminated the ancient and continuous attempt to find some guiding principle in the good, the true, and the beautiful, it may be called nihilistic. In the sense that it lacks even a normal curiosity in the possibility of an interrelated universe, it can be likened to the ancient system of Pyrrho. Pyrrhonism succeeded completely in disengaging itself from intellectual curiosity.

> The unhappy desire to know was the
> cause of all fever and fret, the po-
> lemical passion and the torturing
> doubt. Once grasp that the desire
> was essentially futile, that you could
> let the mind play and *hold it back*

---

[3] Positivism is but one branch of modern critical thinking. A movement so broad cannot be defined in the terms of a single name. Thus logical positivism, logical analysis, analytical philosophy, semanticism, all contribute to the atmosphere of radical empiricism. What holds this diverse world together is not so much their agreement as it is their disagreement. Thus although Bertrand Russell has himself been critical of positivism he stands with positivism against the kind of generalizations that gave Greek philosophy its metaphysical power.

all the while from fixed belief *(epoche)*,
and there was no reason why you should not
be perfectly happy. . . . It was a wonder-
ful deliverance to realize that you
need not mind not knowing. This,
apparently, was Pyrrho's gospel.[4]

Logical positivism, Pyrrhonistic or not, has had a significant influence upon, at least, the university mind. It is
doubtful if any but the academic would be disciplined
enough to enter into its esoteric frame of reference. It is
clearly a philosophy for the intellectually élite. At least
some of its thinkers—Bertrand Russell, for instance—have
been drawn from the ranks of higher mathematics. Though
it has had little influence on art and theology it has stimulated and, in turn, been shaped by the social sciences.

The goal of positivism has been to lift thought from
the subjective to the scientific level. Its method distinguishes
sharply between what can be known and what cannot. With
an almost Puritan rigor it refuses to be tempted into the
ways of the flesh: it will not discuss speculative propositions. Entering into its sparsely furnished cell, it seals itself
off from any of the normal worldly interests in metaphysical,
theological, and ethical judgments.

In agreement with the analytical methods of Plato and

---

[4] Edwyn R. Bevan: *Stoics and Skeptics* (New York: Oxford University Press, 1913), p. 124.

Aristotle, the positivists part company whenever any of the classical thinkers drive beyond the range of their analytical competency. Analyze sense perceptions if you will but, please, no generalizations or inferences about the universe! The cosmos, or any idea which unifies the totality of experience under a single heading, is merely a word: it has no basis in experience except as a loose and inexact generalization.

The radical limits to which inquiry may legitimately be directed may be best illustrated in comparing a positivist with some of the classical concerns. Thus, Plato, in discussing the problem of knowledge, inescapably concerned himself with time and eternity, the good, the true, and the beautiful. The goal of Kant's critical philosophy was to find a way of honoring the analytical method and yet providing some foundation for man's knowledge of God, freedom, and immortality.

Professor A. J. Ayer, one of the most influential of English positivists, has also written a book on *The Problem of Knowledge.* But Ayer's book discusses none of the larger issues raised by his predecessors; in contrast he seems to exploit more pedestrian interests. He is concerned only with the content of experience, the reliability of sense perception and memory. The book closes not with a chapter on God or anything so extravagant as the good, but with the question, *myself and others.* The problem, as Ayer sees it, is simply, can we know anything about each other at all?

Beyond this concern we may not go.[5]

A thinker who was somewhat alien to positivism might charge it with attempting to know more and more about less and less. The positivist could respond that traditional and idealistic followers, by following a noncritical procedure, end up knowing less and less about general categories, the idea of a unified universe for instance. The horizons of positivism seem to be surprisingly limited. Occam's razor, the principle that the extraneous must be separated from the essential, is applied with ascetic ruthlessness. With David Hume, the eighteenth-century patron saint of modern nihilism, positivism has declared the broad range of human concerns out of bounds.

What is the basic premise of the movement? All that is true must be verifiable. What kind of verifiability? To the positivist there can be only one kind, empirical. Corporate experience, universal human belief, cannot be verified by laboratory methods. The world of introspection and imagination is ruled out. Only the world of the test tube and the computer counts. A necessary connection must be established between the hypothesis and the conclusion. Proba-

---

[5] The reader need not hope that Professor Ayer has at this point climbed Mount Everest. No one will ever accuse Mr. Ayer of having made the case for intrapersonal knowledge exactly overpowering. The later analytical thinkers have acquired both more modesty and more diversity in their interests: at the same time the observer detects little interest in how the metaphysicians understand themselves.

bility is not good enough. Certainty is necessary. How much certainty? Not less than 100 per cent.

Given this assignment, what can be known on these precise terms? All that can be known must be both necessary and clear. What are the areas of thought in which necessity and clarity prevail? Logic! Mathematics! What else? Sometimes the word symbols which express . . . language. But not just any language—language which has been purified, purged of confusion, language which corresponds to logic. Actually, language can be understood only if it be guided by the spirit and forms of mathematics.

The positivist is sure that if discipline be maintained, one can say almost exactly what one means. But it doesn't come easily and doesn't come at all if intellectual slovenliness persists. Thus, one must avoid all words about which one is uncertain—truth, good, god, and the like. Who really knows what is meant by the word . . . god? The use of the word adds nothing except confusion. It isn't that logical positivism is committed to atheism. It is merely that the question about the existence of God is meaningless. It cannot be discussed. Thus, says Mr. Ayer,

It is characteristic of an agnostic to hold that the existence of a god is a possibility in which there is no good reason either to believe or disbelieve; and it is characteristic of an atheist to hold that it is at least probable that no god exists. And our view that all utterances about the nature of God are nonsensical, so far from being identical with, or even lending any support to, either of these familiar contentions, is actually incompatible with them.[6]

Thinkers ought therefore to talk only about those realities with which they have direct empirical knowledge. Since neither a unicorn nor a god can be seen, both words should be restricted to their mythological meaning.

It can be argued that positivism seems to be overmuch influenced by the methods of the logician and too little by the creative arts. It almost seems as though positivists take language out of the stammering tongue of the poet and put it into the unambiguous mouth of the scientist. Positivism freely admits its kinship with the world of science. Indeed, the positivist frequently views himself as an acolyte of the laboratory. Therefore, the positivist does not actually create the mighty acts which belong to empiricism. He merely handles the elements of language so that they will be kept free from contamination. Thus according to one interpreter the sole function of philosophy is to

. . . clarify the meanings of words and statements and to identify and eliminate nonsensical statements. Accordingly philosophy does not establish specifically philosophical propositions but only clarifies given propositions. Philosophy is not a system of truths and therefore does not constitute a special science; rather it consists in "that activity by which

---

[6] Alfred Jules Ayer: *Language, Truth and Logic* (New York: Dover Publications, Inc., 1937), p. 115.

the meanings of propositions are ascertained or clarified." Philosophy clarifies propositions, science verifies propositions. The latter is concerned with the truth of propositions, the former, however, with the question what exactly propositions *mean*.[7]

What then is logical positivism? It is an attempt to insure intellectual clarity by insisting upon the verifiability of all propositions. Its concern, as far as the general public understands, has been necessarily with semantics, the clarification of language.

It views with regret humanity's various detours from intellectual respectability. It is not partial in the suspicion that it casts upon these errors. It is no more opposed to the Christian faith in the Incarnation than it is to the Platonic faith in the Good, or the Marxist faith in the development of history toward a just economic and social order. It is prepared to eliminate all these symbols of darkness, symbols which have held man back from his true destiny, clear thinking.

CONTRIBUTIONS OF POSITIVISM

Nonpositivists find it relatively easy to dismiss positivism. In part this repudiation comes easily because to the outsider positivism loses on three counts. It seems to be an unnecessarily arid system, its language is dangerously eso-

[7] Viktor Kraft: *The Vienna School* (New York: Philosophical Library, 1953), p. 188.

teric, and its practitioners seem to manipulate conversations without regard to democratic procedures.

To many opponents it seems as though the preoccupation with the scientific tends to produce too mechanical a kind of thinking. Positivism, in its effort to be precise, fails to do justice to the lyrical dimensions of human experience. There is no more reason that we should think in a completely analytical manner than that we should think in a completely poetical manner.

The fact that positivists seem to reflect a kind of intellectual élite has not encouraged them to attempt a communication with the world's peasants. Indeed, its failure to take responsibility for mass communication reveals a kind of proud homogeneity in the movement. Nowhere are lines drawn so clearly, nowhere does a group make less of an attempt to enter into the terminology of the opposition. Indeed, most nonpositivists have a sense of deep frustration for having surrendered to the stock gambit *what you really mean is*. If the nonpositivist pauses to listen, he soon loses the logic of his own game and finds himself checkmated.

But the fact that positivists seem to express a lack of humility does not justify the opposition in assuming that positivism makes no contribution. It has something to say, especially to those who are involved with the—perhaps more profound but also more ambiguous—dimensions of art, ethics, and theology.

Indeed, in living in a world in which language has been

debased not only by modern advertising but also by politicians and churchmen, it is reassuring to know that there is one school of philosophy which insists by its probing and sometimes insulting questions that man know what he is talking about. Easy generalizations about God, about righteousness, are in danger of becoming a mask for ignorance. It should be required that a man, before he utter, think more painfully about the limits of his language. Only then would it be possible to purge from speech slovenliness and vulgarity. It is illogical to affirm, as many churchmen do, that God has been seen and that he is a spirit. If God is a spirit, he cannot be known through our optic nerves, and it is useless to insist that seeing is meant spiritually, without suggesting that God was imagined. The assault of positivism is necessary for all those who do attempt to communicate the impossible, the notion that all experience is underlined by that which is more than experience.

Logical positivism places upon each man the responsibility of explaining what he means. Gone is the built-in vocabulary. Gone is the reliance on straws, words that had been thought to possess a fixed content. Instead of assuming that ideas exist, it becomes the task of each person to create his own, to fashion his sentences as carefully as a carpenter fashions a door to fit a frame. Ludwig Wittgenstein, professor at Oxford, epitomized the analytical responsibilities of the thinker when he said that *words have usages but never meanings.*

Also, the attack from the realm of logic should remind all metaphysicians and theologians that they engage in an art in which there is no self-evidence. The idea of a unified universe, whether in being or in love, is not one that can be taken for granted. The assertion that the cosmos has meaning is not necessary to logic; indeed, it represents a break with logic. Those who are willing to make that break ought to acknowledge that they have crossed into a more dangerous frontier. They should formulate, more clearly than they have done, the rules by which that frontier can be crossed. Thus all easy reference to faith as though faith were an easy alternative to thinking needs more clarification than theologians have been willing to give. God is not a matter of fact and God cannot be verified. Those who find this proposition difficult ought at least to be grateful to the positivists for communicating a truth even though—and what important truth is not?—that truth is painful.

THE LIMITATIONS OF POSITIVISM

The critics have a right, however, to ask a few questions. The attackers themselves must also live in a world in which they too are robbed of their self-evidence.

What kind of world helped to create a kinship between men like Bertrand Russell, G. E. Moore, and Ludwig Wittgenstein? Two or perhaps three dimensions of the modern world seem to have been especially important in shaping the form of logical positivism.

First, positivism was born in an era which had committed itself to the virtues of the scientific method. It is therefore the child of a technical rather than an aesthetic or religious civilization. Almost born in the laboratory, it has gained from the scientific environment a concern which is unique to the scientific method . . . precision. Born in an other age, positivism might have concerned itself with the creative distortions employed by art, but, instead, it has been marked by its dedication to a gospel of exact measurement. The positivists find themselves completely compatible with the aims and methods of science. Indeed, it could almost be said that a slightly incestuous relationship exists between the two. A scientist who is either a Marxist or a Christian will find an interesting tension between the form of his Idea and the scientific method. A scientist who is also a logical positivist is at rest within himself. Ultimately the lack of tension may cause spiritual death.

Positivism, like so many other branches of the scientific discipline, seems to lack a sense for history. Partly it absorbed from the nineteenth century the confidence that the present was infinitely wiser than the past. The result is that positivism seems to be either unwilling or unable to enter into dialogue with the past. The Renaissance man, Kierkegaard the existentialist, and nineteenth-century German idealists, in addition to developing their respective positions, also conducted a love affair with some aspect of Greek thought. Positivists, however, are perfectly satisfied with their love affair with the scientific method. From their point of view the position seems to be a highly moral one; they do not intend to commit intellectual polygamy. On the other hand, it may also be that their parochialism will prohibit them from entering into a multiple-dimensioned universe.

Positivism seems further sealed off from creative turbulence in that it cannot engage in conversations with its own time. Partly it is in a class by itself: it is the only movement which will not engage in generalizations about experience. It seems almost Victorian in its desire to protect its virtue from contamination. Other thinkers do not consider that it is necessarily immoral for a philosopher to borrow and enrich himself from other positions.

The engineered isolation of the movement seems again to arise because of the almost paranoic loyalty to clarity. Thus Professor Morton White of Harvard reveals the temper of his own involvement when he says:

> It is a remarkable tribute to an enormously muddled but brilliant German professor of the nineteenth century that almost every important philosophical movement of the twentieth century begins with an attack on his views. I have in mind Hegel. . . .[8]

---

[8] Morton White: *The Age of Analysis* (Boston: Houghton Mifflin Co., 1955), p. 13.

This judgment on Hegel was inevitable. It reveals the magnetic attraction that positivism has for positional thinking. If a position has something to say about the universe, if a metaphysical insight is hazarded, the positivists attack. This is no accident since, having studiously avoided any venture on their part, they must demolish those who, whether they succeed or not, make the attempt.

Hegel, that strange nineteenth-century thinker, is a natural lightning rod. No thinker in the modern world has labored more mightily to do justice to the premise of the modern world and simultaneously to keep alive the Socratic-Christian idea. Hegel, probably more than any modern thinker, has contributed to the insight that history represents the fulfillment of a purpose, that culture is the result of the incarnation of a developing power, that all art, philosophy, and theology are themselves the result of the progressive incarnation of the Absolute Idea. Hegel, therefore, reflected the substance of both the Christian and the Marxist conception of history. Both these movements presuppose what the logical positivists cannot, that history is itself a reflection of an ultimate and understandable purpose.[9]

Positivism, in addition to its parochialism, seems to lack

---

[9] Christian readers of this book may be disturbed by the fact that they are continuously linked with Marxism. Yet both Christianity and Marxism reflect a courage to believe that life is the mirror of an ultimate purpose. They have infinitely more in common with each other than they do with the nihilism of positivism.

a critical attitude toward its own methodology. It assumes that the empirical method, the principle of verifiability, is the valid method, the single clue to true knowledge.

The reliance on a single method sounds dangerously as though a disguised metaphysic had crept into the analysis. For no method and no premise can be justified on its own terms. Empiricism can be justified only because the present civilization is interested in the results of empiricism. It, too, like every philosophical method which preceded it, is conditioned by its involvement in a given culture.

Earlier this essay has suggested that creative criticism arises out of a marriage between skepticism and faith. If this thesis is correct, then positivism or analytical philosophy fulfills the function of critical thinking only in part. At best it is a limited corrective method. At worst it substitutes a negative for a dialectical view of the universe.

ORTHODOXY

Pyrrhonism may both be viewed as a constant threat to easy systems of metaphysics, and also be understood as a suicidal attempt to substitute chaos for the cosmos. Orthodoxy, the opposite distortion, can be viewed as a welcome enemy of nihilism and also as a Promethean attempt to substitute a rigid order for the freedom that belongs to the cosmos.

Contemporary forms of religious orthodoxy, like logical positivism, were formed by the collapse of medievalism and the emergence of the modern secular world. Like the originators of the modern scientific method, and like many Renaissance thinkers, Reformation theology attacked the medieval synthesis. Both philosophies created new world views by returning to the original sources. Hellenism has continued to trigger new forms of creative secular thought and the Bible has fired the imagination of a Protestant world.[10]

The sixteenth century saw the emergence of new and powerful forces. Some were political and others were economic. Not the least of these explosions was a marching idea, Luther's recovery of a universe grounded in an ultimate mercy. Many controversies forced the creation of an immense number of peripheral issues, but Luther was most concerned with the announcement of the divine love. The logic of controversy often necessitated, in Reformation thinking, emphasis on such joyless topics as original sin and predestination. These concepts, however, were only pawns on the chessboard. It was the resolute queen, the doctrine of the merciful grace of God, which protected the gospel.

Luther's insight gave man a new vision of himself and his universe. Before the love of God, manifested in Jesus

---

[10] Because Roman Catholic orthodoxy is concerned with restating the terms of the medieval synthesis and because sectarian orthodoxy seeks to disengage itself from the rhythms of secular society it is useful, in this analysis, to concentrate on that form of orthodoxy, Protestantism, which is somewhat more entangled with the modern world.

Christ, the chaos and the darkness gave way to reconciliation and light. The universe was no longer under the authority of malevolent demons but under the gentle righteousness of God.

> Righteousness, then, is such a faith and is called "God's righteousness," or "the righteousness that avails before God," because God gives it and counts it as righteousness for the sake of Christ, our mediator, and makes a man give to every man what he owes him. For through faith a man becomes sinless. . . .[11]

The excitement which this faith created can only be likened to the original proclamation of Jesus, for the message of Jesus that *the kingdom of God is at hand* and the message of Luther that *through faith a man becomes sinless* are the same.

As soon, however, as the secondary forces began to take over, it became apparent that heavy buttresses would be necessary to sustain the magnificent vault of the Reformation faith. Definitions in the form of carefully defined judgments on the Bible, the church, the sacraments, were necessary if the initial joy were to continue. It was not long, however, before the followers were compelled to defend the formula and not the faith. Soon the Reformation began to develop a logic similar to that of the Roman church. In

---

[11] *Works of Martin Luther,* Vol. 6 (Philadelphia: Muhlenberg Press, 1932).

spirit the Westminster Confession, the Augsburg Confession, and the Council of Trent are similar. All three attempt to define the boundaries so that there can be no confusion on the part of the followers of the Reformed, the Lutheran, and the Catholic traditions. Precision of definition had been gained but, as far as Protestantism was concerned, a formula now obscured the vision of the universe which the initial thrust of faith had uncovered.

No seeker after truth today would have the same exhilarating experience that Luther had, if he had first to plow through the literature of Protestant scholasticism which succeeded the Reformation. An orthodox formula, because of the tragic dimension of history, may be necessary but it can only be somewhat anticlimactic to the original excitement.

CONTEMPORARY ORTHODOXY

The orthodox Protestant church today can be defined as that community which is primarily concerned with influencing American culture through the theological confessions established in the wake of the Reformation. Many churches have interests in addition to their orthodox concerns, but most Protestant communions are anxious to read the universe according to the charts of Westminster, Augsburg, and so on.

The nineteenth century, in contrast to the seventeenth,

regained the curiosity which endless definitions had eroded. Protestantism began to examine the relation between its own theological tradition and the vitalities of general culture. Liberalism encouraged the church to pay its respects to the scientific method. The social gospel enabled the church to borrow and transform insights garnered from both Marxism and pacifism. And the twentieth century has seen the emergence of yet another force, the ecumenical movement, which has also enabled the Protestant church to move into wider areas of concern.

Both liberalism and the social gospel expressed a criticism of the *status quo*. Both became instruments of that highest form of criticism, self-criticism. Through liberalism's involvement with Freud, Darwin, and the like, and through the social gospel's involvement with some Marxist and pacifist principles, the church created useful problems for itself. As it struggled with these problems it expressed a bold and a creative tension. Because it could never quite resolve the tension between the gospel and the world, it became dangerously alive.

It is ironic that the present revival of religion in America should take place after the decline of both liberalism and the social gospel. With the insecurities attendant upon the cold war American culture has indicated more and more interest in a religion which would radically distinguish it from the concerns of the Soviet Union. A return to pre-liberal and pre-social gospel orthodoxy has seemed to provide the answer.[12] Protestantism has as a result lost much of its capacity to criticize the social and economic order.

As a result of the vacuum, American culture has witnessed the magnification of enthusiasm and sentimentality and the minimization of criticism. The extent to which Christianity is responsible for cretinizing the mind of the church is illustrated by the statement of a prominent evangelist:

> What is repentance? How long has it been since you preached a sermon on repentance just as you would explain it to a group of children? Dr. Louis Evans, one of our great Presbyterian ministers, said that in his preaching he found that the religious intelligence of the average American congregation is that of a 12-year-old. "I always talk to the people now as if they were children," he added. Dr. James Denney once said, "If you shoot over the head of your congregation, you don't prove anything except that you don't know how to shoot."[13]

In the last analysis there may be little difference between the presuppositions of the modern advertising executive and the Christian church. Both seem determined to keep man at a level which will obscure his inherent dignity.

---

[12] Orthodoxy must be distinguished from that theological movement known as neo-orthodoxy which sat in critical judgment on some of the oversimplifications of liberalism. Neo-orthodoxy, especially as reflected by Karl Barth, is grounded in a skepticism far more radical than any interpretation which has hitherto associated itself with Protestantism.

[13] Sermon by William Graham from *Christianity Today*, p. 3, Vol. III, No. 22, Aug. 3, 1959.

The political insecurity of our times and the easy system of orthodox religion seem to have tailored the world for the appearance of the revivalists of the 1950's. As far as the development of the critical and skeptical traditions are concerned, the emergence of a mass manipulator like Billy Graham is important for three reasons. First, his appeal to the faithful seems to require an abdication of the intellect. In his preaching little attempt is made to illuminate the problems of either the Bible, theology, or faith. Faith solves and eliminates the problematic dimension of human existence. The contours of faith are roughed out with slogans such as *Believe in the Lord Jesus Christ and be saved.* Though every Christian would affirm the centrality of this idea, most would admit that the statement must be placed in a broad and meaningful context and that in doing so, real problems emerge. The dramatic preaching, the public acknowledgment, the decision for Christ, all subvert the intellect. There is little hope that the convert will learn to live in a world in which human wisdom daily loses ground in its race to understand the world's complexity.

Graham, furthermore, makes no attempt to relate the gospel to the creative dimensions of culture. Art, music, the theater, intellectual experience as such are ignored or linked with sensuality and worldliness. Graham is cheerfully prepared to superimpose the moral judgments of an obscurantist on the subtle and creative dimensions of urban culture. It is conceivable that the theater of Arthur Miller and

Eugene O'Neill has given modern man an image of himself which is indispensable for the renewal of his imagination and his humanity. If so, no one will ever accuse Billy Graham of having tried to understand this vein of creativity.

Finally, Graham—and every other revivalist for that matter—gives substance to the judgment of intellectuals that Christianity is a mask for obscurantism. Such an idea makes it difficult, if not impossible, for genuine conversations to take place between Christians who want to think and non-Christians who might want to understand why Christians believe as they do. Without Graham it would be more possible to communicate to the world that mature Christianity is as committed to skepticism as it is to faith, for on the creative interaction of doubt and belief hangs Christianity's contribution to the critical life.

But in order to understand the extent to which the revivalists have destroyed the relevancy of Christianity to culture, it is necessary to understand something of the peculiar content that orthodoxy in its Protestant and Calvinistic form has taken.[14]

---

[14] Although there can be said to be a Lutheran and a sectarian orthodoxy none is so important as Calvinism. Sectarian orthodoxy as represented by the Quakers is perhaps the most insular of all contemporary religious disciplines. Lutheranism, on the whole, has had less influence on American culture; and the ambiguities of Luther did not permit the tradition to harden in quite the same way as did Calvinism. American culture, insofar as it has been affected by a religious tradition, is Puritan and Calvinistic.

Protestant orthodoxy, particularly in its Calvinistic branches, is characterized by a compulsive assumption that faith produces knowledge. Furthermore, this knowledge seems to lack a sense of finitude. In this sense the orthodox mind is the opposite of the Pyrrhonist who sponsors a metaphysical nihilism. One cannot help having the feeling that when one moves from unyielding doubt to unyielding certitude, one has been in the presence of two dangerous dogmatisms.

In contrast to the logical positivists, Harold J. Ockenga, in a sermon preached at the Second Calvinistic Conference, assumes that man possesses an *innate knowledge of God.* Man is furthermore *indubitably* persuaded and he possesses a knowledge of God which is *ineradicable.* Before the exciting but sometimes confusing fabric of biblical insights, the believer can say, *I know.* How can the believer be sure? The Scriptures are *infallible.* The Bible contains *no error of fact.* Indeed, biblical literature is differentiated from all other literature in that it is more *dignified, simple, direct, beautiful,* and *unequaled* in *form.* Mr. Ockenga is supported by Professor Louis Berkhof who declares that Calvinism is the fruit of an *unquestioning faith.*[15]

Lest secular critics assume that these oversimplifications represent the mind of faith, it should be pointed out that

---

[15] *The Second American Calvinistic Conference* (Grand Rapids, Mich.: privately printed, 1943), pp. 25-42.

more mature minds have refused to take man out of his creatureliness by speaking about ineradicable, unquestioning knowledge. The New Testament, for instance, speaks more modestly of faith when Paul says that *faith is the assurance of things hoped for, the conviction of things not seen.* Furthermore, in comparison with the almost neurotic quest for certitude on the part of Mr. Ockenga, the Apostles' Creed possesses a gentle humility. Here is no attempt to create a problemless universe. Instead, "I *believe* in God the Father, maker of heaven and earth, and in Jesus Christ, His only son, our Lord. . . ."

What is orthodoxy? It is a movement which intends to retain the power of the original intellectual and spiritual explosion. It attempts to do this through the definition of that explosion through a series of doctrines. By requiring assent to these propositions it intends to train the individual so that he can take the proper stance when he faces the reality which created the original explosion. The orthodox doctrine is therefore always once removed. It is not the idea but rather the cumbersome apparatus which protects the idea.

THE CONTRIBUTIONS AND
LIMITATIONS OF ORTHODOXY

Both the positivist and the orthodox mind suffer from dogmatism. Yet, except for their mutual inability to criticize their own premises, they differ radically from each other.

Whereas the primary function of positivism is to clarify confused ideas, orthodoxy clarifies very little. Its mandate is quite different.

The strength of orthodoxy is that it combines engagement with compassion. Unlike the positivists it does not declare the broad range of human concerns out of bounds. It involves itself with every dimension of reality and is prepared to make a judgment. From the point of view of modern Pyrrhonism it makes too many judgments. Perhaps! But it is not hamstrung by its own intellectual apparatus: it can evaluate.

In part it is able to engage itself with human existence because it has refrained from being an élite. If its logic is sometimes confused, its aesthetics lacking, its taste vulgar, it is because it has chosen to communicate itself through the masses. Orthodoxy does not make merely Olympian judgments about humanity. It is involved with man. There is no primitivism that it will not face, no danger that it will not stand up to.

This involvement arises from the fact that orthodoxy *is* concerned. It cares about man and his eternal destiny. It is perhaps this compassion which causes it, for the sake of general humanity, to forsake scholarly precision. Truth is understood in a corporate sense. Truth is not the proud possession of the disengaged individual. The fact is that the orthodox mind, through the translation and distribution of the Bible, has probably created greater literacy than any other force in history. While careful and precise scholars are sharpening their tools in isolation, a member of the orthodox community is sitting out in a distant jungle teaching some primitive to read.

The orthodox mind therefore must be appreciated for the manner with which it has built an elaborate machine to educate the world. Perhaps this process lacked subtlety; but, even so, the church has prepared the barren ground so that minds capable of greater subtlety, although not necessarily wisdom, will not need to labor within the range of primitivism.

In building this vast educational and ecclesiastical apparatus the orthodox churches have ministered to a large community. Countless numbers have been given the opportunity of identifying themselves with an empirical community which does communicate the idea that the universe has purpose. Perhaps, although improperly exploited, the backlog of Christian thought has enabled contemporary culture to withstand the daily brainwashing that it receives from the popular media of communication.[16] The church has created a community and has consistently directed the mind of that community toward a ministry to the world, the world of the sick, the imprisoned, and the friendless.

Grateful as history ought to be for the fact that the ortho-

---

[16] It would be a difficult choice if one had to cast one's lot with either secular or orthodox brainwashing.

dox communities have attempted to communicate an Idea, it must be also admitted that that Idea has been frequently mutilated by those who have loved it best. Orthodoxy can be said therefore to be its own worst enemy. Loving the Idea it seeks to perpetuate it somewhat in the manner of a nervous but domineering mother who is determined that the child shall make the right decisions. Frequently speaking of faith the community relies instead upon a built-in response. Orthodoxy is therefore not necessarily, as Dostoevski seemed to believe, the enemy of freedom. It is, nevertheless, always a little embarrassed and frequently suspicious of freedom.

Indeed the compulsive interest in solutions, the crippled interest in questions, tends to press the orthodox mind toward not sensitive faith, but pretentious knowledge. The orthodox mind has never accepted the insecurity that belongs to faith. The assumption that man's mind is clear enough to have a genuine knowledge of God seems to suggest a confidence in reason which is too Promethean. The Pyrrhonists are at least as correct in placing far lower estimates on the power of reason.[17] In any case the confidence in reason fails to do justice to the fact that all true relationships, especially the relationship between God and man, are grounded in a mystery. Furthermore, the mystery is so

---

[17] Calvinism, however, does pay lip service to the notion that man's knowledge of God has been corrupted by sin.

deep that it resists a facile reading and a simple interpretation via a system of doctrines. At best, doctrines are but symbols, partial and maddeningly incomplete. The confidence that the orthodox mind attaches to its apparatus of knowledge obscures its contribution to that Reality which reveals the incompleteness of every rational discipline.

POLARIZATION

Compulsive skepticism and orthodoxy both fail to do justice to the complexity of experience. Both correct each other's distortions, but neither is able to do justice to both creativity and criticism. When these two dimensions are divorced, then man either loses the courage to risk ultimate interpretations of existence or he loses the power to criticize his interpretative compositions.

Each position sacrifices maneuverability for the advantage of a consolidated position. Truth for the dialectical thinker, however, is always a matter of question and answer. Questions that risk no answer, and answers that acknowledge no questions are equally dangerous. Logical positivism has surrendered to a method which seals it off from the possibility of having an answer. In the same sense, orthodoxy is so nervously committed to a fixed answer that it has cut itself off from honest questions. Both speak to the impatient—to those who will not listen to the full story of man's hunger and to the answer provided by a more sensitive reading of experience.

Why, having overcome primitivism, does man make such poor use of his freedom? Why does he insist on living with questions that provide no answers or with answers that presuppose no questions? Christianity, perhaps better than the radical skeptics, understands that men do sin against that reality which they are seeking to interpret and serve. Christians understand less well, however, that they are just as easily victimized by man's tragic capacity to deceive himself.

If man is to live dynamically, he is dependent upon a truth which has the power to stimulate him. At the same time, unless he can escape his tragic fate, he is tempted to capture that truth. As he makes the truth into part of his system, he cages it. When he makes the truth into his system he may note that he is becoming bored but may not notice that this is so because he has gained a jail and lost a universe.

Neither the orthodox nor the skeptics have much cause to cheer. Both have oversimplified. There is, thus, an analogy between the university and the church. Students within the university, faced with all the complexities of relative knowledge, sometimes look with nostalgia upon their childhood in the church. The church had, they feel, something to say. To be sure, it seems that it was said too simply but it was said. The church, on the other hand, looks upon the university as too uncommitted. Which is right? Neither. The church needs the university to save it from obscurantism.

The college needs the pressure of a Christian community—for the college can only clarify: it cannot create ultimate values. Those who lack resiliency, or a sense for the paradoxes of the universe, will seek to escape the tension. So they either discard their religious heritage and settle back into a skepticism, or, tired of endless questioning, they retreat into the church, lock the door, and throw away the keys of criticism.

Are these the only sad alternatives, parochial orthodoxy or empty skepticism? Happily not, and we may look elsewhere to a world view which includes both creativity and doubt; a critical vision of truth which includes both the university and the church. We must now turn away from polarized and incomplete views—away from those who assail and those who protect—to that vision of truth which is the subject of both distortions.

3 | Critical Christianity

LOGICAL POSITIVISM AND PROTESTANT ORTHO-
doxy both have merit. Positivism provides a critical discipline by which language can be clarified. Orthodoxy, on the
other hand, has succeeded in communicating to the average
man the idea of a purposeful universe. At the same time
both positions falter because their dogmatism prohibits each
from interpreting more than a limited facet of experience.
The question must be asked, Is it possible to move beyond
nihilistic criticism or an unimaginative orthodoxy to a position which will maintain a more dialectical understanding
of the universe?

Is there, apart from the polarized societies, a community

which combines criticism with creativity? Is there within the Christian tradition itself a community which is concerned with more than a system of doctrines and which is simultaneously committed to a criticism of its own premises? Are there not, among true Catholics, Protestants, and Jews, some who are prepared to believe that Reality cannot be limited to the sum total of their respective or even of their joint traditions? Such an ambiguous community, if it could create proper safeguards against pretension, might refer to itself as critical Christianity.

It is not to be assumed that critical Christianity is to be limited to those who happen to be creedally secure or doctrinally sound. It includes all who have possessed the humility to hazard a communication. It includes all who have been willing to express their dependency, who have not been too proud to beg or to borrow. It includes all who have been willing to suffer rather than to close the channels of communication. It is expressed by all, whether as atheists or as believers, who have dared to hope even when they could not understand.[1]

The term critical Christianity is not necessarily as divisive as it might sound. It attempts to be genuinely catholic, for it includes the whole community which has been involved in the ferment of the Christian dialogue with cul-

---

[1] Atheism, as the dialogue between Santyana and religion would indicate, belongs within the boundaries of critical Christianity.

ture. It is not limited to the ecclesiastical world. It includes all those thinkers and artists and politicians who were informed by and stimulated by both the Socratic Idea and the biblical Idea. It includes all who struggled to articulate the interrelationship between love and knowledge, who themselves were convinced that the universe was itself grounded in a communicable order and a loving purpose.

THE OLD TESTAMENT

The modern man, schooled in the logic of evidence, necessarily finds the world of the Bible confusing. If he is not careful he is liable to measure the biblical truth in terms of his own parochial assumptions. He may forget that the Bible, originating in a prescientific environment, forged its own unique method of escaping primitivism.

Any attempt to blend modern empiricism, or medieval scholasticism for that matter, with the biblical materials results in artificiality. Thus popular attempts either to validate or to invalidate the miracles of the Bible are doomed to failure. The biblical man, as he created his literature, did not assume those fixed rhythms of nature which have been so essential to the modern view of the cosmos. It is therefore never quite possible to be certain, since he was not conversant with the problem of natural order, what the biblical writer had in mind. Did the original author of the following lines view them as a statement of fact or of a liturgical faith?

Then spoke Joshua to the Lord
in the day when the Lord gave the
Amorites over to the men of Irael;
and he said in the sight of Israel,
"Sun, stand thou still at Gibeon,
and thou Moon in the valley of
　　Ai' jalon."
And the sun stood still, and the
　　moon stayed,
until the nation took vengeance on
　　their enemies.[2]

The author himself does not communicate his own judgment of how the lines should be interpreted. It is therefore fatuous to discuss what did or did not happen since there is no way of knowing even what the writer thought had happened.[3] Christian theology has frequently claimed, in retrospect, that the biblical writers were describing miracles. Perhaps! But it is always easier to make a miracle retroactive than it is actually to predict the future.

Whereas the scientific method stands or falls upon its

---

[2] Joshua 10:12, 13.

[3] *This* contemporary writer, on the assumption that man's experience with nature is uniform, is convinced that the modern world provides better clues to the workings of nature than did antiquity. Every orthodox effort to show that modern principles of indeterminateness validate the biblical material always sounds somewhat contrived. From the point of view of the assumptions of modern empiricism, it would seem that the Bible makes a greater contribution to a poetic than to a scientific understanding of the universe.

[70]

ability to predict, the biblical writer has little interest in prediction. Partly, since the center of Israel's life is found in the Exodus-Event, this is because Israel is oriented toward the past and not the future. Partly this is because the Old Testament man understands reality corporately and not individually, confessionally and not factually. Thus, theology is used to shape memory rather than to analyze the laws of God. The child becomes a member of the community not by testing its assumptions but by sharing its faith.

> "And you shall make response before the Lord your God, 'A wandering Aramean was my father; and he went down into Egypt and sojourned there, few in number; and there he became a nation, great, mighty, and populous. And the Egyptians treated us harshly, and afflicted us, and laid upon us hard bondage. Then we cried to the Lord the God of our fathers, and the Lord heard our voice, and saw our affliction, our toil, and our oppression; and the Lord brought us out of Egypt with a mighty hand and an outstretched arm, with great terror, with signs and wonders; and he brought us into this place and gave us this land, a land flowing with milk and honey.' "[4]

[4] Deuteronomy 26:5-9.

The modern man, unless he neutralizes his own bias, will not be sensitive to the nuances within biblical thought. Even when Amos seems to point to the coming destruction of Israel he is not predicting an event in the modern sense of the word. Isaiah who looks forward to the day when *the wolf shall dwell with the lamb* is delineating not an event whose birth can be measured but rather is testifying to a world of mercy ultimately more meaningful than the normal political world. No attempt is made to control or even suggest the interval before the event is to occur. The prophet thus always speaks out of his hope and not his knowledge.

The Hebrew is asked to trust God in order to avert the wrath which is to come rather than to live through the wrath in order to find out whether the prophet's accuracy could be measured.[5] The Old Testament, or the New Testament for that matter, is not involved in an empirical examination of nature and history. A dynamic relationship between God and man is presupposed but no one claims to have "tested" that relationship.[6] When the biblical man faces God, he faces him not as a manipulator but as a suppliant.

Just as the biblical mind must be distiguished from that of the scientific mind, so too must it be differentiated from

---

[5] Amos 5:15.

[6] It must be admitted, however, that the later Apocalyptic literature begins to manipulate time. The author of Daniel comes close to predicting the day of God's intervention.

that of the primitive mind. The scientist because of his own parochialism too easily identifies every method other than his own with primitivism and superstition. Actually it is possible to escape from the prison of primitivism in a variety of ways. The Greek dramatists, Aeschylus and Euripides, did it as effectively as the more abstract thinkers, Euclid and Aristotle. In the same manner the biblical man also charts his own unique form of escape from primitive slavery.

The biblical man did not win his freedom through scientific objectivity. He found another and, perhaps, richer road to freedom. Like the scientist, he understood himself to be neither the manipulator nor the dumb extension of nature. Unlike the primitive man, he possessed a sense of his own separation from the powers which confronted him. He existed as a spiritual being. Spirit was not understood, however, as an additional faculty, but rather as an added dimension to man's psychology. This dimension of spirit comes into existence in the moment when man realizes that he is more than an extension of his environment, that in some sense he is responsible for himself. Though he always remains a part of nature he now finds himself required to make decisions that do not seem to have originated in nature.

This movement into spirit is, as Kierkegaard saw, one of *fear and trembling*. Spiritual man is akin to the adolescent who discovers that he is neither an extension of the family nor is he quite free. On the eve of freedom he tastes both the joy and the dread of freedom. Until he stands before the abyss and looks into the mist hoping to see his own image, he is not a person. However, as soon as he leaves the womb of nature or family or tribe, he becomes aware of the fact that he is disengaged. He is independent and dreadfully responsible.

Primitive man, struggling with the apparent malevolence of nature, attempted to control those arbitrary powers by sympathetic magic. By the infinite personalization of natural forces he sought to control and direct the action of nature. But unlike both the modern scientist and the biblical prophet, he did not understand the sovereignty of the forces which confronted him. He assumed that he had the power to manipulate. He believed that there was a direct cause-and-effect connection between his totems, his ritual, and the responsive action of the natural world.

The scientist does not, of course, assume that he has any power over nature. He stands patiently before the complexities of nature's laws in a humble effort to understand and, understanding, to redirect the human response. He may set the laws of nature in opposition to each other, but before those laws he is a supplicant and not a god. As such, the scientist is a person, has a sense of personal existence because he knows the boundaries that separate him from the world which he is trying to understand.

The biblical man also knew what it meant to stand apart from his reality. Although there are vestigial remnants of magic in the literature of the biblical peoples, the Old Testament represents a decisive break with a magical conception of nature.

Unlike the Canaanite faith which it supplanted, the biblical peoples did not attempt to control the deity through fertility rituals, incantations, and the like. Indeed there seems to be strong evidence which indicates that the steel of the Hebrew faith was sharpened on the flint of Canaanite magic. The awful sense of the sovereignty and holiness of God in the Old Testament only makes sense as a reaction against a dreadful sense of "togetherness" between man and God in the womb of a nature religion.

In primitive magic the priest and the instruments of his power are central. The saving word comes from the lips of the priest. His incantation is indispensable, because only through it can the demon-god be controlled.

The biblical man, like the scientist, found himself in a reversed situation. All his priests were demoted. They became merely liturgists and celebrants of the communities' relations to God. They offered prayers but not incantations. Power was transferred from the priest's lips to the Director of the Universe. As the saving word is placed in God's mouth man becomes a listening, receptive being. His authority, analogous to the empiricist's understanding of nature, demands that the priest or clan magician be deposed. It is God who now saves, and all that the religious apparatus has left is its ceremony.

The reduction of the authority and status of the priest underlines the finitude of the religious leader. Thus the prophet informs the nation that

> "When you come to appear before
>   me,
> who requires of you
> this trampling of my courts?
> Bring no more vain offerings;
>   incense is an abomination to me.
> New moon and sabbath and the
>   calling of assemblies—
> I cannot endure iniquity and
>   solemn assembly.
> Your new moons and your ap-
>   pointed feasts
>   my soul hates;
> they have become a burden to me,
>   I am weary of bearing them.
> When you spread forth your hands,
>   I will hide my eyes from you;
> even though you make many
>   prayers,
>   I will not listen;
>   your hands are full of blood."[7]

With the demotion of the priest-god, Israel had no alternative except poetry; and thus the prophet came into his own. So Israel passes from magic to literature.

---

[7] Isaiah 1:12-15.

Disengaged from the artificial authority of logic and science, the Old Testament writer is prepared to exploit a different medium. When he is discussing law, chronology, and merely threshold history he is capable of writing with normal attention to order. On the other hand, when he comes to a more puzzling problem, the meaning of history, the Hebrew writer discovers that a new medium of communication is required.[8]

Whenever man's relationship to reality is involved the writer is forced to move from the directness of logical communication. Thus, whenever an ultimate statement is made, it is not made in the form of a proposition but in the form of a . . . story. The Hebrew cannot talk about God except he talk about Abraham, Isaac, and Jacob. The patriarchs and Moses all take their place, no matter which of the early epicists are talking, as works not of historical research but as works of art. This does not mean that they were invented, but that the Hebrew early discovered that the real must be filtered through the imagination.

The centering of knowledge in the imagination rather than in reason created pressures which shaped Israel's entire world view. From the beginning to the end Israel was, a priori, bound to mistrust any logical formula whether sacerdotal, political, or doctrinal.

---

[8] One of the most creative contributions in this area is found in *The Hebrew Iliad,* by William G. Pollard and Robert H. Pfeiffer (New York: Harper & Brothers).

Israel was faced with the same temptations that blocked the other ancient peoples from apprehending a world unified by intelligent and moral purpose. Faced with the overpowering forces of nature, Israel, in contrast, however, to other Near Eastern peoples, refused to surrender. Like the Canaanites the Hebrews could have surrendered to a system in which natural forces would have been deified. Perhaps in the beginning they did, since the early literature contains remnants of an animistic faith. However, what made the Hebrew faith distinctive was its insistence that the facts of natural existence were not facts but were a part of a unified order, the order of a Creator's purpose. So it was that a later writer summed up the ruling a priori of Israel's life: "In the beginning God created the heavens and the earth. The earth was without form and void, and darkness was upon the face of the deep."[9]

God was to be found only across the formless void. He is not to be identified with anything on this side of the abyss. To find God on this side of chaos was to taste the most terrible emptiness of spirit, idolatry. He who remains in safety and says that he knows God, *feeds on ashes*.[10] God is to be found across the boundary of freedom. He who will not cross the desert, he who hides within the secure walls of the city, knows only an idol.

---

9 Genesis 1:1.
10 Isaiah 44:20.

He who dwells beyond the frontier cannot be caged within the human mind. As the Hebrew writer developed the sense of the abyss, he necessarily laid the ground for critical thinking. God could not be known by direct examination. The Creator—and here the biblical faith is one with modern skepticism—could not be measured by his creature.

As a result of this abyss, this inability to view God as a thing within the cosmos, the Hebrew was saved from the identification of his political organization with ultimate purpose. God was not the state, and above all he was never an official of the state. Israel's theology gained classical form largely as a result of the prophetic reflections on the distortions which were inherent within political existence. Amos, Isaiah, and Jeremiah, in struggling with the problem of the monarchy, were forced to place true power outside of the rights of the kings. Unlike many other Near-Eastern cultures, Israel did not worship its kings. Indeed it was inevitable that the king, like the priest, should eventually lose significance.[11] God was more than a thing, an incanting priest, or a nervous prince.

---

[11] Karl Barth, Europe's storm-creating theologian, has interpreted the Virgin Birth stories to signify that God, in creating the Messiah, was compelled to leave Joseph out, because Joseph, as the male principle, symbolized the kings of this earth. Such a view is, as a poetic image, conceivable because of Israel's strong spiritual allergy to "kingship." It was Lord Acton who with great theological perceptivity summarized the traumatic experience of Israel with its kings when he said, "Power corrupts and absolute power corrupts absolutely."

Most significantly, the resistance to idolatry saved the Hebrew from—in the sense in which the term has been used in the preceding chapter—becoming orthodox. Just as the priest and king were demoted, so too were theological propositions. The biblical writer, because of his involvement in the art of poetry and the epic, did not anticipate the later Western reliance upon a system of doctrines. The law of noncontradiction is meaningful only to those who have sought to impress upon the universe an ultimate and unyielding consistency. With a strong sense of the limits of direct analysis, the Hebrew was prepared to recognize that the tension between justice and mercy was ultimately more meaningful than a tight doctrine which would eliminate the tension. From the point of view of the biblical man, Christian insistence upon assent to propositions about God represents not an extension of the biblical faith but a bastardization of Aristotelian logic and Western views about the Bible.

The Hebrew thus developed a conception of reality which saved him from ever quite identifying his own concepts with that reality. Whatever was thought had first to cross over the abyss of the imagination if it were to communicate something of God. The combination of a mistrust of logic and a creative sense for the abyss enabled the Hebrew to think afresh instead of merely codifying his experiences.

Even a casual examination of a prophetic writer will reveal the exciting way that he permits the burgeoning tides of life to inundate and reshape his thought. Thus facing one situation the Prophet Hosea can imagine God saying, "I will destroy you, O Israel; who can help you?"[12] And yet on a different occasion the poet can visualize God saying, "I will heal their faithlessness; I will love them freely."[13] Neither Hosea nor the other poets felt that it was their task to provide a fixed unity for these images. They were receptacles for the brooding spirit of the universe, not its editors.

It is this poetic freedom which, since Christian theologians are more logical than poetical, is so frustrating to the postbiblical interpreter. Christian theology desires, because of its analytical interests, to define God. It seeks to find the essence of his behavior, to rob him of all arbitrariness. The result is, of course, systematic thinking, a disease from which the Hebrew did not suffer.

Happily the Old Testament was not edited and made consistent by a Western mind. It is filled with exciting contradiction. It speaks of God both anthropomorphically and as a spirit.[14] Innocently the imagination moves between the law and grace of God. God is thought of as the Lord of history while history is sometimes thought of as a meaningless rhythm.[15] Thus Amos can hold that God will cause

---

12 Hosea 13:9.

13 Hosea 14:4.

14 Genesis 2:8 and Genesis 1:1ff.

15 Isaiah 45:1 and Ecclesiastes 3:24.

"justice to roll down like waters, and righteousness like an everflowing stream."[16] Later the author of Ecclesiastes can affirm just the opposite: "Again I saw all the oppressions that are practiced under the sun. And behold, the tears of the oppressed, and they had no one to comfort them!"[17]

Any creative writer who has found himself inhibited by the idea of a universe already completely blocked out will find himself stimulated by the freedom of the biblical world view. He will also discover why it is that the Bible is so much more interesting than the Christian theology which attempted to interpret it.

The Hebrew poet did not build up confidence in his power of conceptualization. He knew that the order and content of his mind was never a direct reflection of the reality across the barrier. Freed from an idolatrous reliance upon his concepts, he developed a flexible faith instead of a fixed doctrine.

Contemporary Christian theology has only recently begun to realize why it was that the biblical man developed a unique epistemology. Emil Brunner and Martin Buber especially have allowed this dimension of Hebraic mind to influence them. Both have stressed the fact that man is related to reality, not analytically, but conversationally. All theology, as the ancient Hebrew believed, is dialogue: therein lies its imprecision and its richness.

---

16 Amos 5:24.
17 Ecclesiastes 4:1.

Thus the Old Testament thinker is a skeptic by virtue of the fact that he is a believer. By breaking with magic he was forced to develop his imagination. Through the use of the imagination he was enabled to discover that reality was never identical with priests and kings, systems and doctrines.

Skeptical of both the content of experience and his own head, he developed the courage or the faith that both positivism and orthodoxy lack. He was able to create images and to conceptualize his vision of the universe without making his constructions into a closed system. Freed from magic through a reliance on imagination the Hebrew anticipated the dynamics of a later and more sophisticated age which sought to achieve a balance between creativity and criticism.

THE NEW TESTAMENT

Christianity, an amorphous and multicultured movement, has never been entirely happy within the limits set by the Old Testament. The earliest major heresy, that of Marcion, separated the God of the New Testament from the God of the abyss. The majority mind of the church, perhaps somewhat reluctantly, recognized that it was precisely the radical separation between God and man which distinguished the Hebraic world view from that of paganism.

Christian theology, because of its centrifugal movement toward abstraction, tended to orbit into a vacuum. Its connection with existence has been maintained because the form of the New Testament communication, like that of the Old Testament, is through the refractions of the imagination rather than through a direct and analytical knowledge of reality. The reader of the New Testament will be disappointed if he reads with the expectation of finding some system of knowledge. He will be excited, however, if his mind, in tune with the art of the New Testament, allows the fragments of a vision, its stories and letters, to stimulate his courage so that he can look toward a boundary too subtle to be seen by the rigid eyes of logic.

Nowhere is the contrast between the classical and the biblical views more dramatic than between Stoicism, the heir of the Platonic world view, and Paul, the heir of the Old Testament. Although the two institutions which embodied these views were parallel to each other, the Roman Empire and the Christian community, each was relatively oblivious of the other, each lived by its own past.

Paul, on the borderline between biblical and abstract thinking, illuminates the form in which the earliest Christian community thought. Indeed, Paul is probably more responsible than any other Christian for helping the church to find some epistemology other than analytical reason. As a child of the Old Testament Paul is neither an empiricist nor a pre-scientist. He has little concern with evidence. Therefore he influences the life of the community toward a different kind of knowledge when he says:

[84]

We know that the whole creation has been
groaning in travail together until now;
and not only the creation, but we ourselves,
who have the first fruits of the Spirit,
groan inwardly as we *wait* for adoption as
sons, the redemption of our bodies. For
in this *hope* we were saved. *Now hope that
is seen is not hope.*[18]

Here we find a theology not built upon a spurious claim, or
a claim that represents a labored logic, but a theology which
has itself been constructed upon the corporate hope of a
community.[19]

Stoicism, on the other hand, was convinced that the universe moved by a clear rhythm of natural law and that the
human mind was capable of being tuned to that rhythm.
Paul, and the biblical world also, believed that the universe
existed, that man faced a meaningful order. However, what
the Christian community did not believe was that the mind
represented an easy instrument by which the secrets of
that order could be read. Reality was separated from man
by a barrier which could not be crossed by the analytical
mind.

---

[18] Romans 8:22-24 (Italics mine).

[19] Both pagan and Christian readers will be aware of the fact
that Christianity is frequently unwilling to live by so fragile an authority as . . . hope. Christians, like others, become easily fatigued
with the demands of creatureliness. They have been known, especially
in the pulpit, to invent evidence.

According to the New Testament, God's will knows no reason which is accessible to man; his judgments are unsearchable, and his ways are past finding out.[20]

Unlike Stoicism the New Testament places no great confidence in the power of human reason. Like the Old Testament its creativity is grounded in a critical and skeptical attitude toward direct knowledge. Like the Old Testament it is required to communicate its conviction not on an argument but on the impact on the human imagination.[21]

There is a kind of refreshing candor to the claims that the New Testament makes. Thus, Paul admits that the Christian position has little wisdom to be said for it.[22] He himself seems to be rather easily bested in arguments with Athenian philosophers.[23] The Messiah in whom Paul places his hopes is, like Socrates, destroyed by the forces which he has challenged. Jesus, however, lacked a Plato and comrades who might have given dignity to his death. He died repudiated not only by the world at large but, most ignominiously, by his closest friends.[24]

---

[20] Rudolf Bultmann, *Essays* (New York: The Macmillan Company, 1955), p. 76.

[21] It is true that Paul does, from time to time, engage in a curious kind of argumentation. See Romans 13:1-7. But in this area, compared to the Greeks, Paul is a child. His contribution comes rather from his personal commentary on a story which the community well knew, the story of the crucifixion of Jesus of Nazareth.

[22] I Corinthians 1:20-31.

[23] Acts 17:16-33.

[24] Mark 14:50.

In spite of the fact that after a generation, a community did emerge in support of this strange and gentle criminal his biographers described him as lacking in all the virtues which would have attracted the ancient man. He is spoken of as both cursed and foolish.[25] This description is given not by his enemies but by his friends and disciples.

An observer could not help thinking that the New Testament was not exactly putting its best foot forward. This is no accident since the Old Testament conception of the abyss between man and God forces the New Testament writers to heed this limit. Thus knowledge is never used in the New Testament in an analytical sense. Knowledge is always understood in a personal sense and communicated in a dramatic sense. It is frequently equated with an intuition of integrity,[26] associated with the limits of human knowledge.[27] It is expressly stated that man cannot know who the Son is.[28] Indeed, in view of the fact that man is of the world he cannot know God.[29] When knowledge is used as a characteristic of man, it usually implies belief or conviction, both of which represent man's limited form of knowing.

If the New Testament, like the Old, takes the division be-

[25] Galatians 3:13 and I Corinthians 1:23.

[26] Matthew 7:23.

[27] In Matthew 13:11, knowledge of the secrets of heaven is a gift and not an achievement.

[28] Luke 10:22.

[29] John 1:10.

[87]

tween time and eternity seriously and radically, why then does it not end up in Pyrrhonism? How then can it provide a dramatic vision which suggests the unification of experience into a universe? How then can there be any concord, to paraphrase Tertullian, between Jesus and Socrates?

The New Testament does not, in spite of its skepticism, collapse into intellectual defeatism. Although man cannot substantiate the universe, the New Testament adventurously affirms that the universe, the world of meaning, substantiates man. While analytical reason cannot cross the crevasse, while reason cannot accomplish the traverse, while the space seems to become emptier and emptier, the New Testament world discovers that what man sought to do and could not do had already been done. God had crossed the abyss.[30] Thus knowledge, in its truest sense, is available. It belongs to him who successfully accomplished the leap, God. Only the Lord God knows your hearts.[31] It is not man but God who knows.[32] Man cannot himself cross the pass but he does know the love which passeth knowledge.[33]

---

[30] The word *abyss* does not of course come from the New Testament. The reader may suspect that it was lifted from Paul Tillich. Perhaps! At the same time the reader is asked to remember that the equivalent is to be found in the New Testament conception of the *stumbling block* and the contradiction between the wisdom of God and the wisdom of the world. See I Corinthians 1:18ff.

[31] Luke 16:15.

[32] Galatians 4:9.

[33] Ephesians 3:19.

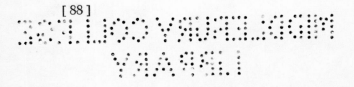

If it is God who knows, and not man, then what is the source of human conviction? Conviction always represents knowledge which is finite, limited, and uncertain. At its highest it can be only hope: it can never include certitude. Here the New Testament is closer to the logical positivists than it is to the metaphysicians. In short, it anticipates the problem of skepticism, honors it because of its own conception of creatureliness and then, utilizing another instrument, attempts a breakthrough to a new vision of the universe.

It should now be clear to the reader of these essays that there is an irreconcilable and therefore creative tension between art and argument, the Bible and logic. Any reader who wants to test this tension can do so by reading the heavy and overly victorious logic of either Calvin or St. Thomas Aquinas with the more aesthetic and elusive insights of the Bible.

Nowhere is the nonanalytical dimension of the Bible more dramatically illustrated than in the Gospels. Here is a world farthest removed from propositions that can be tested, most irrevocably immersed in the world of imagination.[34] As the reader turns to the most intense of all dramas,

---

[34] Theology almost invariably functions by the following rule. The more a believer feels compelled to *explain* faith the more necessary it is to use rational and logical language. On the other hand, the more faith is *described* the more necessary is the language of the stage, poetry, the novel. Only the language of the drama allows the writer to communicate indirectly, to allow his reader to participate in the relationship which is being described.

the story of the life and death of God's carpenter-son, he observes that the scene opens with the following words: "The beginning of the gospel of Jesus Christ. . . ." The use of the word gospel, which literally means good news tells the reader that he is to hear not a chronology of events but a dramatic message, a story which will communicate good tidings.

The gospel is a unique literary form. It is neither a literary invention nor an organization of fact. It represents the wedding of history and imagination, the union in Greek terms of Herodotus and Euripides. In this sense the writers of the Gospels continue to rely on that unique boundary form, the story of Exodus, as the means of communicating a truth which is more than but not less than fact.

The stories of the Exodus and the life of Jesus express an ultimate courage and a deep creativity. In telling these stories men were able both to address the universe with their hopes and to use the story as a mirror in which to measure human destiny. Whereas the Old Testament attempts to communicate the story of every individual through the account of a corporate experience, the New Testament attempts to communicate corporate destiny through the life of a single individual.

The epic of the New Testament, although necessarily foreshortened, contains the same ingredients of imagination, the same creative distortions that were reflected in the story of the escape from Egypt.

The Gospels communicate a vision, not a laboratory demonstration. The Gospels tell of the drama of faith: they do not attempt to prove that faith. The writers of the Gospels conduct no arguments, marshal no evidence. The movement is not from hypothesis to proof. No attempt is made to demonstrate that the conclusion is necessary. The writers of the New Testament are not research assistants collecting data. The lineage of the writers is in the saga and the epic. It is inevitable, therefore, that the gospel, like every other drama, can speak only to those who are themselves caught up into the drama. To those who stand aloof, to those who insist upon comfortable objectivity lest they risk the anguish of their own transfiguration the gospel has nothing to say. The gospel is tellable but not measurable.

The knowledge of God is again communicated from lips to ears and not within the silences of the mind. A book which purports to be of God tells about . . . a crucified criminal. The radical juxtaposition of the highest that man can think with the lowest that he can experience forces a problem into existence. Why when man wants to think of *eternity* must he look at *time?* Why when he seeks for *life* must he look at *death?* Why when his heart hungers for *peace* must he observe a *crucifixion?* Why when he wants to think about *God* must he read about a *carpenter?*

Pagans, even since the Renaissance, have been happy to discover that the Bible reflects the human in all its contradictions. Orthodox Christians have been depressed because they have had to pretend that the problem does not exist. But the problem is itself essential to the story. The problem is the threshold over which the reader must cross if he is to understand the narrative.

The Christ of God is not easily come by. God's carpenterson is communicated only through a drama, a drama whose first task is to destroy the artificial security of the reader. When the drama takes hold—any drama—the onlooker is lifted out of his chair and transported to the road before him, there to suffer, there to believe and disbelieve in the glorious torment of existence. All true art is the enemy of apathy. The gift which the art of the gospel gives is turbulence of spirit.

He who reads the drama of the Gospels, according to their literary form and not according to preconceived prejudices, discovers that he is thrust immediately into a critical relationship to that which he is trying to understand. The Gospels thrust their problems into the mind of the reader: they are not hidden.[35]

_____

35 Although it was the modern world, primarily the world of Wellhausen and Streeter, which has created the tools to analyze the synoptic problem, even the casual reader of the New Testament is forced to make some judgment about the agreements and the disagreements in the four Gospels. The fact that the order of events in Matthew, Mark, and Luke seems to be quite different from that of John, the fact that each Gospel seems to have its unique interpretation of the import of Jesus forces the reader to create some theory which will account for the differences and agreements in the narratives.

Pyrrhonism and orthodoxy demonstrated that through polarization it is possible for man to avoid the pain of a critical position. The biblical man, however, neither denied contradictions nor did he exploit them in order to deny their intent; for the biblical man, because of his own sense of the abyss, knew that contradiction was not an accident, but that it was at the heart of the biblical affirmation.

Perhaps only the postbiblical man can appreciate the full force of the critical problem created by the Bible. It is the tension between art and logic which forces criticism. Just as the creative artist and the art historian are in conflict, so, too, are the biblical writer and his postbiblical interpreter. Nowhere is the conflict more apparent than in the clash between the Aristotelian's conception of an orderly world and the biblical exploitation of disorder as the context of meaning. When Western man "examines" the miracles of the Bible he must either deny that the miracles were facts or affirm that they were facts born because, under the aegis of the Creator of natural law, law itself was temporarily placed in abeyance. However, this question, either in the form of an apologetic for a fixed and unyielding natural law or for a natural law which knows an occasional truancy, is irrelevant to a people who told the miracle stories without knowledge of a problem which had meaning only for a later era. The stories cannot, therefore, be forced, without being made to lose their art, into a counsel for the defense for a more sophisticated world. They must be taken as they stand, as the art by which the community communicated to itself the cosmic drama of redemption, the battle between God and Satan.

The reader finds gathered around the person of Jesus a drama similar to the drama of Job. The person of Jesus suggests to the continuing community that in the Messiah-Event God had overcome Satan. The miracle stories make this faith vivid and communicable.

Only orthodoxy with its lack of artistic imagination could make the drama into a set of rules about natural law. Only nihilistic skepticism could feel emancipated in proving that the Gospels could not be taken literally. It is almost as though the artistic form of the Gospels represents an anticipation of such polarization. If so, then the most serious errors ever committed have been so done by those who have either blindly defended or attacked that which they had not the humility to understand.

Even more than the letters of Paul the Gospels communicate a delicate hope to minds that are prepared to take the risks of sensitivity. Their ingredients are neither security nor knowledge. The stories of the Gospels reveal the imagination of those who had the daring to cross frontiers that were alien to their intellectual routines. The Gospels were not written by men who were willing to be immobilized because they had to know precisely where they were.

If the writers of the New Testament did not limit their

curiosity to a world which they could measure, it is due to the fact that their chief subject, an apprentice carpenter, seems to have had unusual powers of imagination.

Like the earlier prophets, Jesus broke with traditional forms of communication. He engages in no catechetical training of the memory. Nor do his disciples learn through recitation. Unlike the orthodoxy of his day he does not engage in humdrum homilies on traditional ideas. Instead, he creates through a highly sensitive art form, the parables.

His dramatic parables, analogous to contemporary short stories and poetry, are memorable. The parables of the Good Samaritan, the Prodigal Son, and the Pharisee and the Publican have shaped the channels of Christendom's imagination.

The parables, like every true form of art, are never conventional. Their meaning is suggested but never fixed. They are explosions into freedom. The parables are the mirrors to a shifting, shimmering idea. They represent a marriage of meaning and mystery. Lacking the obvious, they lay a bold demand upon the sensitivity of the hearer.

Jesus seems to be incapable of making an obvious remark. Rather he tells parables in which he expects his listeners to find the truth. Having told his story Jesus frequently closes with the words: "He who has ears, let him hear."[36]

---

[36] Matthew 13:9. According to the account of the early church (Matthew 13:10ff), Jesus explains the parables to the disciples. The movement from a demand of the imagination to a pedestrian explanation

Only he who ventures into freedom can understand the stories of Jesus. He creates freely without a dull formula. Nor does he feel compelled to edit and remove the contradictions. Sometimes he tells of the endless love of God, sometimes of the radical moral judgment that God makes upon sinners. No attempt is made to provide a framework, no attempt is made to remove the rough edges of reality. Jesus through a multiplicity of insights communicates an illumination rather than an organization of the universe.

Jesus was an exciting thinker for whom form was as important as substance. Actually as in every other great thinker the form cannot be separated from the substance. It was the marriage between form and substance which gave classic power to his idea. And it was the form of the parables which enabled Jesus to make his most decisive attack upon the intellectual obscurantism of his own day.

The obscurantism of Pharasaic Judaism was not much different from the obscurantism of later Christian orthodoxy. Judaism and Christianity are continually plagued by a heritage which is rich enough to force the present to become an insignificant appendage of a glorious past. The tension

---

can make sense as an addition of the church only as it tried to communicate to itself the reasons why the minority had understood Jesus, and the majority had not. Actually such an explanation robs the disciples of their dignity, and makes it appear that they acted without faith and risk and simply on the basis of some secret information. It is probable, however, that Jesus was closer to an artist than he was to being a kind of celestial tipster.

between Jesus and the pious organizers of the past is illustrated by the following dialogue:

> "Why do your disciples not live according to the tradition of the elders, but eat with hands defiled? . . .
> Well did Isaiah prophesy of you hypocrites, as it is written,
>> 'This people honors me with their lips,
>> But their heart is far from me;
>> in vain do they worship me,
>> teaching as doctrines the precepts of men.'
>> You leave the commandment of God and hold fast the tradition of men."[37]

The artistry of Jesus is dedicated to communicating the single insight that the ancient God of Abraham is the living Lord of the present. His first sermon was that *the kingdom of God is at hand*.[38] And his stories and parables are developed always to show that God is not the prisoner of antiquity.

It is not that Jesus repudiates the past. It is merely that by creating new forms of speech, he shatters the synthetic authority with which truth is obscured by the varnish of antiquity. Jesus insists that those who live in the present

---

[37] Mark 7:5-8.
[38] Mark 1:14.

must live as dangerously as did those who lived in the past.[39] In order to emphasize the power of God in the present, however, he frequently sounds as though he were setting the past against the present.

> "You have heard that it was said, 'You shall not commit adultery.' But I say to you that every one who looks at a woman lustfully has already committed adultery with her in his heart."

> "You have heard that it was said, 'An eye for an eye and a tooth for a tooth.' But I say to you, Do not resist one who is evil. But if any one strikes you on the right cheek, turn to him the other also."[40]

This dualism is only apparent, however. What he does is to undermine the authority-barnacled rules of the past so

---

[39] A sociological examination of the material in Mark 21:15ff will indicate that whereas Jesus himself seemed to have observed most of the traditions, except that he did heal on the Sabbath, his disciples were, from the point of view of the orthodox, culpable. Jesus seems to have drawn his disciples from what the Victorians would have called the lower classes, fishermen, tradesmen, etc. Jesus himself seems to have felt that religion could not demand of men what they were culturally unable either to understand or to produce. Jesus ruins the identification of social class with a religious community, and he seems to have created a heartwarming precedent for such few churches today who are ashamed to exist merely because they constitute a vault into which the hopes of middle-class and suburban selfishness can be locked.

[40] Matthew 5:27 and 38.

that men will create new rules relevant to the present. At times he seems to deny all rules insisting that before God man cannot measure his responsibility. How much does God demand? Merely everything!

Eager to relate man to the abyss of God directly, Jesus freely moves from paradox to paradox. Thus, on the one hand, he emphasizes love, "Judge not, that you be not judged,"[41] and, lest this be made into a manageable rule instead of a reflection of the chaos before which man must stand before he faces God, Jesus says:

> "Do not think that I have come to
> bring peace on earth; I have not come to
> bring peace, but a sword. For I have come
> to set a man against his father, and a daughter
> against her mother. . . ."[42]

Jesus seems to be more interested in seeing what happens to man when he approaches the chasm than he is in rule keeping. Therefore, his demands push rules to their breaking point and thereby drive man deeper and deeper into the problem of his own existence. Or the reader is told, in the story of the return of the Son of man, that those who do not feed the hungry, welcome the strangers, clothe the naked, visit those who are in prison, will be sent into eternal punishment.[43] The reader, following the positive as well

[41] Matthew 7:1.

[42] Matthew 10:34.

[43] Matthew 25:31ff.

as the negative side to this passage, might be tempted to believe that he has discovered a difficult but possible series of ethical prescriptions which will enable him to get ahead. Heaven and eternal life certainly seem to be worth the concentrated attention to the sick, the hungry, and the prisoners that this text seems to demand. But before the reader becomes too enthusiastic over this bargain he remembers the problem of the man who seemed to have lived just such a good life.

> " 'God, I thank thee that I am not like other
> men, extortioners, unjust, adulterers, or
> even like this tax collector. I fast twice
> a week, I give tithes of all that I get.'
> But the tax collector, standing far off, would
> not even lift up his eyes to heaven, but
> beat his breast, saying, 'God be merciful
> to me a sinner!' I tell you, this man went
> down to his house justified rather than the
> other; for every one who exalts himself
> will be humbled, but he who humbles himself
> will be exalted."[44]

Doing good under certain conditions seems to be absolutely useless and not doing good if properly and honestly responded to seems to be a truer relationship to God. Or to put it far too simply yet dramatically, the message of Jesus seems to be that *if a man does the good in the wrong way*

---

[44]Luke 18:11ff.

he is doomed, but if he does evil in the right way there is hope. Thus speaking of a prostitute Jesus said:

> ". . . I tell you, her sins, which are many, are forgiven, for she loved much; but he who is forgiven little, loves little."[45]

Facing those who have frozen the divine freedom into a set of rules, Jesus presses these rules to the point where the whole system collapses. Thus, he informs the young man who has acted as morally as explicit rules can guarantee that he must

> ". . . go, sell what you possess and give to the poor, and you will have treasure in heaven; and come, follow me." When the young man heard this he went away sorrowful; for he had great possessions.[46]

The disciples are obviously confused by this seeming betrayal of a fixed ethic. They are astonished, they despair. If a traditional ethic cannot save, who then can be fulfilled? But Jesus assures them that once the protective barrier of rules have been removed, God can do what the rules cannot: "With men this is impossible, but with God all things are possible."[47] Nothing is fixed. Life and relationship are mobile. The dullard who lives in an easy routine has missed the good news. It requires agility to understand this elu-

---

[45] Luke 7:47.

[46] Matthew 19:21-22.

[47] Matthew 19:25f.

sive gospel. And the agility means spirit, criticism, struggle, resistance to all easy systems, to a system of clear but irrelevant rules. Jesus thus pushes man, like the prophets before him, into a new boundary in which again he is forced to raise skeptical and critical questions about his own powers, his own system, and his own understanding of reality. Jesus drives his disciples into a new relationship to all that has seemed self-evident, to tradition, to institutions, and to rules. The disciples are thrust into . . . freedom.

The insistence that traditional religion had to risk the dangers of the present created an exciting tension from which, happily, Christianity has never successfully recovered. Because Jesus refused to hide the present in the past the abyss was inescapable. From henceforth, Christianity notwithstanding, Jesus had created an intriguing space between God and custom.

Both the form and the content of the New Testament guarantee that the reader will be exposed to the critical problem. Indeed, perhaps to circumvent the dangers of systems like orthodoxy and Pyrrhonism, the critical principle is made explicit. The thrust of the literature drives its readers to the point where doubt itself is included within the normative category of understanding.[48]

---

[48] Again the reader needs to be warned lest he confuse legitimate anguish with methodological doubt. The reader is asked to determine which is the more profound, the implicit doubt in Kafka's *The Castle* or the somewhat contrived doubt of Descartes.

There are many illustrations which demonstrate the integrity of doubt. Peter, the foremost of the disciples, is described with a refreshing lack of heroism. In fact he is honored even though he denied his lord. Thomas is allowed full membership in the community even though he doubts:

> "Unless I see in his hands the print of the
> nails, and place my finger in the mark of
> the nails, and place my hand in his side
> I will not believe."[49]

What is even more important is that *no one censures either Peter or Thomas, and one is given the impression that doubt and an honest skepticism are a normal part of the life of the community.* If this is so—and all the evidence points in this direction—it can be only because Jesus in his manner and attitude included a basic honesty within his affirmations. Jesus does not seem to have been contrivedly pious, and although he articulated some of the profoundest hopes that a living sentient being has ever uttered, he seemed capable also of expressing doubt. On the cross Jesus is understood to have whimpered, "My God, my God, why hast thou forsaken me?" What Jesus meant by these words, or what the disciples thought that he meant may never be entirely clear. What is sure, however, is that they could not have been spoken or recorded had the writers, like the Stoics, possessed a view of human nature which required

---

[49] John 20:25.

an invincible courage. Both the Old and the New Testament accept human weakness and both assume that man's knowledge, like his virtue, is incomplete.

A world which had not been tempted to attribute divinity to man found human fragility to be no problem: man remained human precisely because of the abyss. Furthermore, the awareness of that abyss influenced the form of his communication. The man of the Bible did not see himself in the clear mirrors of sculpture: he heard himself, rather, in the passing echoes of language. Unlike the more spatialized Greek, he developed little sculpture and architecture. Almost all his energies went into words. Freed from both the heaviness and the lucidity of marble, his mind was shaped by the moving, singing sound of nouns and verbs; for, as sculpture trains the mind toward clarity, so does language direct man toward mystery. Lacking holy things,[50] his mind was shaped by poems and parables. Living in an audible instead of a visible world, his spirit was oriented toward creative uncertainty.

Living close to the power and uncertainty of sound, the biblical man was driven toward a world which was neither secure nor nihilistic, the boundary of truth. Indeed, the art of the whole Bible is directed toward exposing man to an inescapable boundary. He is forbidden fixed knowledge so that he can develop his imagination. And his imagination

---

[50] Holy things are not only sacerdotal objects but also things which possess divine beauty.

is ultimately directed toward a contradiction, toward the abyss of the Carpenter of God. Through his faith he reaches out toward the abyss knowing that he will find God or . . . emptiness. On such a gamble the Christian faith was founded.

4 | *Christian Cultures*

THE TRANSITION FROM PRIMITIVISM TO CIVILI-
zation was made possible by a double vision. From both
the Hellenic and the Hebraic worlds man received the idea
of a cosmos. From them he also received a predisposition
toward critical thinking.

Out of the creativities of the Athenian Academy and
Hebrew poetry the medieval, the Protestant, and the contemporary world have fashioned the institutions which
have, skillfully or awkwardly, communicated both the Idea
and the Critical Method. By and large the church has become the spokesman for the doctrine of an integrated universe, and the university has become the homeland of criti-

cism. At the same time, as the analysis will indicate, the method and the idea cannot be divorced. The university therefore also lives by a faith that it can never make quite explicit, and the church lives only when its subjectivity is chastened by disciplined thinking.

The two great religious cultures, Catholicism and Protestantism, have been able to endure only because both of them, sometimes with more reluctance than grace, have created new critical methods to accompany the forms in which they have cast their views of the universe.[1]

The religious cultures of Catholicism and Protestantism would not have been able to make this contribution had not both been dependent upon an earlier and infinitely more dangerous venture. Between the worlds of the Bible and the great medieval synthesis so clearly defined by St. Thomas Aquinas occurred a bold amalgamation of ideas, the scale of which has never been surpassed.

---

[1] Both Catholicism, that monument to medieval civilization, and Protestantism represent creative distortions of the Idea which they have so uniquely communicated. Both represent the courage to amalgamate the Idea with the new cultural forms that were emerging. Had either remained static the church would have become a comical sect instead of a magnificent venture of faith and error, courage and pride, compassion and pretension. Even the dreadful mistakes of the church have reminded it that it does not and dare not live in a vacuum, that error is eternally the companion of faith. The church did not choose to protect its intellectual and spiritual virginity. Thus the monuments of medieval and modern culture represent Christianity's contribution not to the truth but to the dialogue by which the truth is shaped.

The early church faced an unnerving experience which could have forced it into infantilism but which instead precipitated it into intellectual maturity. Early in the second century the church discovered that the initial excitement of the apostolic faith was losing its luster. Those who had known and who had been able to communicate the strange and exciting power of Jesus were all dead. All that was left were some writings and an oral tradition. Separated from the focus of its reality by the passage of time the church began to lose its purpose. Dissension and schism, attempts to create an external authority, tended to dim the light which had been brought into the world. In this awkward moment the church, insecure and peripheral, had to examine its relation to the world at large.

Some thinkers, the author of the Didache, for instance, were content to expand and develop a dualistic or apocalyptical attitude toward culture. Tertullian also saw an insurmountable barrier between the two worlds. Thus, with a certain combination of vitality and obscurantism he could say:

What indeed has Athens to do with Jerusalem? What concord is there between the Academy and the Church? What between heretics and Christians? Our instruction comes from "the porch of Solomon," who had himself taught that "the Lord should be sought in simplicity of heart." Away with all attempts to produce a mottled Christianity of Stoic, Platonic and dialectic composition! We want no curious disputation

[108]

after possessing Christ Jesus, no inquisition after enjoying the Gospel! With our faith, we desire no further belief. For this is our palmary faith, that there is nothing which we ought to believe besides.[2]

Many insecure Christians ever since have attempted to protect themselves from the difficult task of relating their faith to general culture, but happily the mind of the early church was formed by more courageous and less insular thinking.

Some peculiar grace gave thinkers like Justin Martyr, Athanasius, and Augustine the courage to face the best that paganism had to offer and, both shamelessly and faithfully, to appropriate insights which in the end strengthened Christianity and saved it from being deflected from its purpose.

The great strengths of biblical thinking had provided it with its most dangerous flaw. The biblical imagination, to use the language of Martin Buber, had conceived of meaning primarily in terms of the relation between the *I* and the *Thou*. It had spoken with magnificent insight regarding the relation between man and the universe which stood against him. It had, however, never quite succeeded in escaping from its own primitive understanding of nature. Thus Professor Bultmann, perhaps the most imaginative New Testament scholar that the modern world has produced, has

---

[2] Tertullian: "Prescription Against Heretics," Chap. vii, *Ante-Nicene Fathers* (Buffalo: Christian Literature Publishing Company, 1885).

rightly said that the New Testament man thought of the cosmos primarily in terms of man and God and not the universe as such.[3] It is for this reason that the biblical world has a view of nature quiveringly unstable. Thus the strangely malevolent order of nature typified by the New Testament's demonology represented a capitulation to chaos rather than the ordering of a cosmos.

Had Tertullian and the other dualists won the day Christianity would never have been able to borrow from the Greeks the power to take the cosmos out of quicksand. The slow but creative development of Western science could never have been built upon the thin reeds of the Bible's understanding of natural order.

Many thinkers chose a way quite different from that of Tertullian. Thinkers like Justin Martyr saw, as had the Stoics, a clear rhythm in the universe. Even so conservative a thinker as Athanasius could not help affirming that the universe is ordered by the word of God in much the same way that the conductor of a chorus directs the separate members of his ensemble.[4]

The grace to play the feminine role, to receive the thrust of pagan knowledge, was also a matter of necessity. The church, separated from the biblical event, found itself self-conscious over its separation. It found itself in the situation

---

[3] Rudolf Bultmann: *Essays* (New York: The Macmillan Company, 1956), p. 77.

[4] Athanasius: *Against the Heathen. Nicene and Post-Nicene Fathers,* Second Series, Vol. IV (New York: Christian Literature Publishing Company, 1892), p. 29.

in which it could either retreat into ignorance or move forward into a dangerous but exciting learning.

How dangerous that learning was, is evidenced by the fact that many who went this road lost their way and ended up as heretics. Indeed, the heretic is frequently the one who, because of courage, overshoots the mark. Nevertheless, the church attempted to strike a balance between heresy and obscurantism. Its task was to appropriate the strengths of paganism without losing the spirit of its own enterprise.

What were the strengths of paganism? We have seen that the pagan mind, as distinct from the cluttered primitive mind, sensed that the universe was understandable because both the universe and the mind were tuned in to the same order. And it was just this sense of order that the church needed if it was to understand its own freedom. In appropriating order, the church discovered that it lived on a different dimension of history than had the biblical peoples.

Thrust out of the immediacy of the biblical world the church was forced to become the archivist and the judge of its true background. The more it had to define the boundaries of the Bible, the more it had to measure the correct language of faith, the more it had to stand *outside* of that faith. And in standing outside of faith there was no ground available other than the historical principles and the philosophical disciplines of Hellenic culture. Without pagan principles of thought it is unlikely that the church could have translated its creatively chaotic faith into a relatively fixed and communicable form. The Bible, strictly speaking, has no creeds. At least it has no creeds other than liturgical ones. But the early church, faced with heresy, needed an instrument by which it could measure (or claim to measure) correct versus incorrect faith. The great creeds, especially those of Nicaea and Chalcedon, enabled the church to appropriate definitive language in order to insure an exact and scientific measurement of its belief.[5]

The definition of canon and faith, the employment of classical language, meant that the church was now in fact more than an extension of the biblical community. By the employment of pagan tools for its own ends it had declared to itself that truth henceforth must be understood in at least two dimensions, the truth which God had given to his

_____

[5] The Nicene Creed "fixes" the church's mind regarding the relationship of God to Jesus. Seeking for an unequivocal term the church was forced to use the word *substance*. No matter how necessary the definition was, it changed the art of the Gospels into the logic of Aristotle. The psychological pressures upon the church must have been tremendous when it was forced to lose its innocence. Forced to become an archivist of its own history, forced to recognize that it was only the secretary of an earlier encounter between man and the universe, the church was forced to recognize that although it could remember the encounter, it was, like paganism, only indirectly related. The fact that the church has frequently resisted this indirect role should not obscure the fact that more often than not it has accepted its limitations with moderate humility.

people and the auxiliary truth which he had built into language and logic.

In mediating between its own faith and pagan language the church implicitly defined a new conception of human existence. To be human meant not certitude but approximation, not security but living faithfully and dangerously upon the boundary between two worlds.

In taking this dangerous and yet creative venture, the church fathers guaranteed that the ages to come would have a far richer heritage, a heritage of philosophical and critical skills, than if the church had chosen to remain securely within the Bible, hermetically sealed off from that larger world which the God of the Bible had also created.

MEDIEVAL RELIGION

Medieval religion, like contemporary Protestantism, was bifurcated. On the one hand, the instruments of definition forged by patristic theology were given greater scope and authority. On the other hand, thinkers like Duns Scotus, the mystics, and the primitives maintained an interest in a more direct method of apprehending reality, in a method undiminished by rational measurement.

Medieval religion and its child, contemporary Roman Catholicism, therefore represent a synthesis between the logical and the poetic. Both these dimensions are found in St. Augustine, that most creative African thinker, who shaped so much of later medieval thought. Indeed, Augustine is perhaps a perfect example of the synthesis, of the early church's refusal to be driven into a polarized view of existence. His analysis in *The Trinity* represents one of the most careful and abstract definitions that Christian theology has produced. The philosophical and dialectical qualities of Augustine's thought were enough in themselves to make him into a doctor of the church. However, better known, and perhaps far more original, is his *Confessions*. Here the poetic and the nonanalytical triumph as Augustine actually creates a new *literary* form. In this book selfhood becomes an instrument of the literary imagination as Augustine makes a highly introspective autobiography into a tool of theological communication. The reintroduction of the self into theology, in the spirit of Jeremiah, meant that a principle of freedom had been added to the principles of order and logic. Unlike Tertullian, he was able to reintroduce biblical art without repudiating classical principles of order. E. K. Rand, in his *Founders of the Middle Ages*, holds that even though Augustine lacked an interest in Roman civilization, he, nevertheless, through his interest in Virgil, introduced an interest in the classics to the later medieval mind. Thus in spite of Augustine's suspicions regarding Rome he was instrumental in seeing that "Christianity, after much searching of heart, had adopted the ancient culture as part of its own."[6]

---

[6] Edward Kennard Rand, *Founders of the Middle Ages* (New York: Dover Publications, Inc., 1957), p. 280.

[114]

Providing a form for both classicism and the Hebraic heritage, Augustine permanently wedded imagination and order, mystery and analysis. In many ways Augustine was related to medieval theology in the same way that Homer was related to the rise of classical Hellenic philosophy. The journey of the soul from the God which had created it through the world and then home again was as exciting as the long journey of Odysseus.[7]

Just as Augustine is the enemy of polarization and easy systems, so, too, is he the father of ambiguity. The medieval world under his tutelage was prohibited from relapsing into either a completely logical or a completely lyrical method. Both were required, and thereby the mind of the Christian thinker was pressed out of innocency into tension and ultimately into criticism.

---

[7] It is interesting to note that Augustine reverses the logic of that Platonism to which he is so indebted. Whereas Plato sought to eliminate poetry in order that thought could proceed without distortion, Augustine, by his marriage of art and logic, saved for Christianity the possibility of two- instead of one-dimensional thinking. Werner Jaeger in his monumental study of Greek culture, *Paideia: Ideals of Greek Culture* (New York: Oxford University Press, 1954), Vol. III, p. 35, significantly holds that "Plato himself held that the value of Homer's poetry was immediately diminished by a proof that it did not tell the truth . . . and it was the Christians who finally taught men to appraise poetry by a purely aesthetic standard—a standard which enabled them to reject most of the moral and religious teaching of the classical poets as false and ungodly, while accepting the formal elements in their work as instructive and aesthetically delightful."

ANSELM OF CANTERBURY

The centuries following St. Augustine experienced the blunting and rusting of that intellectual instrument which he had so effectively sharpened. It was in this period that the church all but forsook intellectual existence in order to evangelize the northland, the world of the barbaric Franks and Goths.

The barbarian soil on which feudalism was to grow had, like the earlier Hebrew culture, possessed its own rich legacy of myth and poetry. What it lacked, however, was anything akin to a philosophical tradition. Consequently feudalism's mind was never radically disciplined by a sense of indebtedness to abstract and analytical reason.

The mind of the early church had been to some extent shaped by the fact that in order to communicate with the classical mind, it had had to assume an interest in the rational tools which had created classical culture. The early middle ages saw the church, in its conversations with the barbarian world, take on a far darker intellectual coloration. One finds in this period few parallels to the creative and disciplined thinking reflected in Augustine's discourse on *The Trinity*. Instead, the student of this period discovers that the mental faculties of the church were exercised largely through unimaginative and tedious commentaries on the biblical books and, for that matter, on Augustine himself.

Anselm of Canterbury has frequently been called the father of scholasticism.[8] He thus stands with all those thinkers, including Augustine and Aquinas, who were convinced that the chief task of theology was to define the human reason so that its contributions to faith might be understood. Not content with homilies on faith Anselm insisted that the formulations of faith need not and should not be protected from the scrutiny of reason and logic.

In his *Proslogium* Anselm offered a rational argument for the existence of God which has perhaps received more commentary than any other such argument conceived by the mind of man.

> Hence, there is no doubt that there exists a being, than which nothing greater can be conceived, and it exists both in the understanding and in reality. And it assuredly exists so truly, that it cannot be conceived not to exist. For, it is possible to conceive of a being which cannot be conceived not to exist; and this is greater than one which can be conceived not to exist. Hence, if that, than which nothing greater can be

---

[8] The Protestant world, partly because of its own defensive provincialism, has viewed the ideas of scholasticism with poorly concealed contempt. Protestantism, having committed itself to knowledge through faith, has failed to develop a doctrine of the reason. It has seemed therefore to Protestantism that scholasticism's effort to establish the correct relationship between reason and faith is misguided. Perhaps! But Protestantism is not altogether disinterested and at least it must be said that Protestantism is wrong in having almost successfully expunged scholastic thought from the respectable areas which could legitimately concern the Protestant mind.

conceived, can be conceived not to exist, it is not that, than which nothing greater can be conceived. But this is an *irreconcilable contradiction*.[9]

The conclusion then follows:

There is, then, so truly a being than which nothing greater can be conceived to exist, that it cannot even be conceived not to exist; and this being thou art, O Lord, our God.[10]

Many philosophers, including Kant, have since criticized this proof for the existence of God. Being or existence, according to the standard criticism, is not necessarily the predicate of an idea and consequently God's being is not guaranteed by man's idea of Him. Perhaps the criticism is correct. In a final sense every ultimate truth can only be risked: it can never be guaranteed.

It is possible that the criticisms of Anselm have failed to do justice to his thinking on two counts. In the first place, the general context of Anselm's thought assumes that reason can understand the premises of faith but not that reason can validate them. He was far more interested in exploiting the harmony between reason and faith than he was in reducing faith to logic. Second, few of the critics note that the *Proslogium* combines logic with confession. It is significant that *the argument ends in a prayer*, "this being thou art, O Lord."

---

9 Anselm: *Proslogium* (LaSalle, Ill.: Open Court Publishing Co., 1948), Chaps. II and III.

10 *Ibid*.

What Anselm seems to be doing is to bring two worlds as closely together as possible, the two worlds being the *therefore* of logic and the *I believe* of poetry. Indeed in many ways the *argument and confession* of the *Proslogium* represent a most sensitive synthesis of man's double existence, his logic and his faith.

By setting two worlds together, Anselm has avoided polarization. The world of reason has been related to the world of faith, and his word to the thinkers that followed encouraged the development of a theology which dared to think and to believe and to insist that belief enriched thought even as thought disciplined faith.[11]

THE FLOWERING OF THE
MIDDLE AGES

It is in St. Thomas Aquinas and in the poet Dante, however, that the medieval world expresses its most creative union.

Anselm had renewed and reinvigorated the intellectual courage of the Augustinian stream. This stream, however, rapidly dried up; and, although Augustinian Platonists dominated the intellectual scene, by the thirteenth century it was clear that new resources of intellectual criticism were

---

[11] Actually the people who are disappointed in Anselm are the ones whose thinking is itself routinized, who do not accept the dialectic of art and logic, who insist on one or the other. There is little evidence that Anselm thought so suicidally.

necessary. The Augustinian capital had depreciated partly because the mystics, men like Pseudo-Dionysius, had implied that it had been counterfeit. Then the church found itself confronted with a new adversary, a Mohammedan, Averroës, who in rediscovering Aristotle, in effect, declared that Augustine's coinage, following Plato, had been struck at the wrong mint.

The medieval church had the courage to reject the repudiation of reason which the mystics seemed to have advocated.[12] It had the further audacity to allow its own Augustinianism to be revised by accepting the thrust of Averroistic Aristotelianism. It was Thomas Aquinas, the thirteenth-century Dominican, who separated the slag of Averroism from the pure metal of Aristotle. In recovering the insights of Aristotle, he combined a new interest in the life of reason with the more imaginative content of faith.[13]

Like Anselm, Thomas was convinced that reason could and should be related to the life of faith. Unlike Anselm, however, Thomas did not accept the Platonic assumption that the reason possessed a direct connection to an eternal and transcendental world. Thomas, in utilizing Aristotle,

---

12 Mysticism, as distinct from most Western philosophies, tends to depreciate the distinction between subject and object. The loss of the self in reality weakens if it does not destroy the role of the reason as an examining agent.

13 The reader will remember that "imaginative" does not mean imaginary or invented but rather refers to the poetic and storied substance of the biblical vision of truth.

was enabled to come closer to the biblical epistemology which assumes that man knows only as a psychsomatic being. The Platonic thinker had been compelled to bypass sense as an obstacle to knowledge. Platonically speaking, sense was the source of all error and confusion. Only the pure reason could know the truth.

Aristotle, however, had resisted Plato's radical separation of the eternal forms from the actual things of human experience. Instead, Aristotle had argued that the eternal form and the thing were always together. As such, knowledge involved experience with the thing as well as with an intellectual apprehension of its interior being.

The substitution of Aristotle for Plato meant that the thought could not enter eternity by separating itself from the flesh. Man could not therefore have a direct knowledge of God. Thus St. Thomas wrote:

> To know that God exists in a general and confused way is implanted in us by nature, inasmuch as God is man's beatitude. For man naturally desires happiness, and what is naturally desired by man is naturally known by him. This however is not to know absolutely that God exists.[14]

From this denial of a *natural* knowledge of God Aquinas moves toward a defense of a *demonstrated* knowledge of God. He produces five proofs for the existence of God, the most important of which is the argument from motion,

---

[14] Aquinas, *Summa Theologica,* Qu. II, art. i.

or causality.[15] The substance of the argument is that all motion is grounded in some antecedent cause and that the explanation of the origin of motion can come only from concluding the existence of a prime or first mover. It is, says St. Thomas, "necessary to arrive at a first mover, moved by no other; and this everyone understands to be God."[16] On this foundation, always recognizing that man must demonstrate God's existence rather than to know a priori his mysterious essence, St. Thomas builds a picture of man's knowledge of God's unity, goodness, and the like.

He does not presuppose that since man cannot know God's mystery except through His revelation, reason can produce such knowledge on its own as is given to faith. However, he does insist that reason has a role, that it can

---

[15] The Thomistic emphasis upon demonstration or logical proof means that man cannot talk about God unless he organizes his mind. Demonstration means that knowledge does not occur in a vacuum. Man cannot talk about knowledge as though it were as slovenly an act as a grunt or a feeling. Whether St. Thomas meant that reason could conclusively prove God's existence or whether he meant that conversation about the existence of God involves the mind in the act of proof is and always will be a matter of controversy. Nevertheless, as far as the critical method is concerned, the requirement of demonstration fortunately eliminates that cloudy doctrine behind which the uncritical mind hides, self-evidence. In any case, natural knowledge for the modern man means something more direct and less analytical than it does for the followers of St. Thomas. Demonstrative knowledge is closer to the meaning of Aquinas.

[16] Aquinas, *Summa Theologica*, Qu. II, art. iii.

exercise its power creatively in regard to the central meaning of the universe.

St. Thomas is not saying, as many of his Protestant critics seem to think, that man storms heaven. Rather he seems to be saying that the whole of the human personality must be involved in man's knowledge of God. Reason is not exempt: it cannot be allowed to rust in the back yard while faith consorts in the front yard with the angels.

Aquinas has no confidence in a compartmentalized world, a world of faith occupied with one zone and a world of reason with another. Man must think and believe as a unified being. What he says theologically must be said in conjunction with the reason: his theological judgments are not hidden.

This does not mean that reason can censor the judgments of faith, but only that faith in consort with reason refuses to depart from its true task by engaging in nonsense, subjectivity, or tendentious special pleading.

St. Thomas' position, especially if measured by Protestantism's almost total emphasis upon faith, may seem to be too rational, too divorced from the total knowledge that the Bible associates with personality. Perhaps. Certainly his writing and definitions seem to reflect a great concern with abstract versus—in spite of Maritain—existential knowledge. The reader searches in vain for some lyrical passages. None exists. The *Summa* is a monument not to poetry but to order.

However, it must be recollected that the heart of Aquinas' writing is in his conception of the intuition of being. Everything else that he has written is an adumbration of this intellectual faith. Thus, "What is grasped first of all is being, the understanding of which is grasped in every apprehension."[17] Actually the *Summa Theologica* consists of a complete description of the order through which intuition works. Indeed, it must be said that the mind of St. Thomas represents a continual, although not always explicit, dialogue between his premise and his demonstration, between *intuition* and *order;* or that, in other words, St. Thomas reflects the ancient tension between *art* and *poetry,* between *confession* and *argument.*

Nevertheless, most students of the medieval world will find themselves aggrieved because Aquinas' exercise of the imagination is only implicit. Happily they can turn to that poet whose mind was so decisively shaped by Thomas. For Dante, the creator of the *Divina Commedia,* gave the world all the beauty that man could ever hope to see incarnate.

Actually the student would understand the dynamic of the medieval world best if he could address himself to the admittedly superhuman task of reading simultaneously the *Summa Theologica* and the *Divina Commedia;* for just as St. Thomas discovered the lost Aristotelian world of order Dante recovered a lost dimension of Augustine's art.

---

[17] *Summa Theologica,* I, II, Qu. 92, art. iii.

Dante recovers the "Homeric" principle of the Augustinian *Confessions*. Indeed, with complete artistry, almost un-
hampered by the artificialities of abstract thought, Dante
returns not only to Augustine but to the lyrical world of
Abraham and Odysseus.[18] For according to these artistic
spirits man's knowledge of eternity is gained through a
journey. In the migration of the soul through the Inferno,
through Purgatory to Paradise Dante repeats with medieval
vigor the movement of Augustine's soul through the world
to God, of the children of Abraham through Palestine to
eternity.

Happily Dante, like Thomas, Augustine, and the patristic
theologians, had an ambiguous view of the universe. Although the *Divina Commedia* is a lyrical monument to
faith, he cannot make the logic of that faith absolute. Just
as Augustine betrayed the influence of Plato, and Thomas
that of Aristotle, so too Dante refrains from destroying the
classical world. Thus, Dante, because of his love of Virgil,
found himself bridging the abyss between the classical and
the Christian world. As an artist *and* a Christian he uses but
does not surrender to rigid logical rules. Thus the journey
of the soul through the Inferno toward its eventual destina-
tion is guided by a pagan, the poet Virgil. Furthermore, he
separates the sinners from the pagans and gathers the

---

[18] Dante did not read Greek, and therefore his connection with
Homer was always indirect.

philosophers and the other poets into a neutral zone, the limbo or gate of hell. The inclusion of these citizens in an area different from that of the miserably damned indicates the creative ambiguity in the mind of Dante. He communicated the catholic order of the universe but insists that the universe must be read poetically as well as logically. He thus illustrates what happens when monolithic logic receives the baptism of poetic fragmentation. In Dante one finds the highest form of Christian insight, the compromise of dogma by art.[19]

Thus Christendom came to a new point in the development of its critical life. The initial marriage between Hebraism and Hellenism had united the creativities of skepticism and faith. When the patristic church created its first explicit critical principle it recognized that its own life was not identical with the truth which it was attempting to proclaim. With the emergence of a canon and creed, the church was forced to recognize that it had to *think about that which the biblical man had experienced.*

The medieval world heightened criticism by adding the tension between art and logic. Augustine and Dante reintroduced the principle of imagination and thus enabled the church to include within its own vision the truths of distortion as well as the truths of logic. In St. Thomas and

---

[19] The uniting of the world of Paul and Virgil reinforced an earlier apologetic which had prepared the way for a theology of culture.

Dante the reader can see the creative struggle between an analytical structure and aesthetic insights, between a necessary system and the equally necessary shattering of that system.

Thus, medievalism underwrote the initial tension between faith and skepticism with a further ambiguity. By combining aesthetics with logic the church further insured dialectical vision. Not only was man thus able to chasten his parochialism and to find a more complex universe but—perhaps more important—he was able to see the deep universal rhythm between imagination and thought, vitality and order.

THE MODERN WORLD

Christendom, when it was prepared to face the creative tension at the heart of its history, attempted to live on the boundaries of both art and analysis. Though any given individual might, and did, sin against one or the other, the culture as a whole had attempted to express a dual vision of the universe. The danger was not in the synthesis, but in the possibility that the form in which it was cast would become atrophied.

From this danger medievalism did not escape. Over several centuries it demonstrated its inflexibility regarding the cumulative truth of ecclesiastical weaknesses. These weaknesses were emphasized by the fact that the church had allowed its universal vision to become eroded by the provincialism of a landlocked feudal economy. Many forces, including the desire for greater trade and wider communications, called forth a reformation; and with the union of these forces the medieval world disintegrated. The idea of the Holy Roman Empire, the authority of Aristotle, the feudal economy, and the ecclesiastical authority of the Roman church collapsed.

The Renaissance and the Reformation, those forces most easily generalized, had in common an impatience with the failure of medievalism to take seriously the fact that the synthesis had enervated the vitalities which it had attempted to communicate. Medieval culture's easy manipulation of the past, its failure to communicate the original terms, meant that it soon ran out of spiritual and intellectual capital.

As a result, the enduring contribution of both the Renaissance and the Reformation was that they each attempted, before they had to face the problem of their own decay, to return to those vitalities which medievalism had obliterated.

The continental Reformation created three main streams of Protestant thought: Lutherans, Calvinists, and Anabaptists.[20] What was characteristic of each group was its unique

---

[20] Anabaptists, perhaps most unfamiliar to American Protestants, have historically represented an emphasis upon peace and sometimes upon withdrawal from the everyday acquisitive society in which most mundane Christians are prepared to live. The group that fits loosely into the Anabaptist tradition with which Americans are most familiar is the group known as Friends or Quakers.

insistence that reality could be found neither within the synthesis nor within medieval and ecclesiastical history. Lutherans and Calvinists insisted that real history, the locus of time and eternity, could not be found within ecclesiastical history, that ecclesiastical history was only an interpreter of a reality within which it could not dwell. The Anabaptists, thinkers like Menno Simons and Balthasar Hübmaier, insisted that true community could never exist under the jurisdiction of princes, not even the princes of the church. Rather that real history would be found in a radically new history under the aegis of the Holy Spirit. Each wing of the Reformation hungered for a purer and truer world than institutional religion had produced.

Meanwhile Renaissance thinkers, some of whom had anticipated the breakdown of medievalism by hundreds of years, also insisted upon a return to a more direct and less contrived experience with the universe. Both Giordano Bruno and Marsilio Ficino found it possible, like the ancient Greeks, to converse with the universe more directly. Bruno surrendered to a lyrical pantheism, while Marsilio Ficino eagerly threw aside the obstacles of sacerdotalism, sin, and so on and, without these traditional guarantors of individuality, saw a union between man and the universe.

To conclude, our soul by means of the intellect and will, as by those twin platonic wings, flies toward God, since by means of them it flies toward all things. By means of the intellect it attaches all things to itself; by means of the will, it attaches itself to all things. Thus the soul desires, endeavors, and begins to become God, and makes progress every day.[21]

By denying the necessity of an intermediary, Renaissance thinkers both attacked medievalism and reintroduced paganism to Western civilization.[22] Thus the recovery of a direct involvement with the universe plus the Protestant insistence that true history was pre-history or biblical history, meant that together Renaissance and Reformation figures communicated a new and intriguing appetite for reality, a concern for the Idea which could not be identified mechanically with the medium by which the Idea was to be communicated. Both forces gave creative impetus to man's search for a cosmos, a cosmos which could not be reduced to man's laborious records of the order that he had perceived.[23]

---

[21] Ficino, "The Soul of Man," *Renaissance Reader* (New York: Viking Press, 1953), p. 391.

[22] The reader will recollect that paganism was characterized by its innocent directness as it attempted to relate the mind of man to the universe. Christian readers will perhaps consider that the elimination of the abyss, though the sign of sin for the Christian, is for the pagan rather the sign of his courage and his creativity. Had Socrates had a doctrine of original sin, it is doubtful that he would have made the important contribution that he did.

[23] Protestantism, unfortunately, soon fell in love with its own insight. As a result, although it gave lip service to the idea that pre-history occurred before its own history, in its heart it assumed that its piety practically represented a continuation of the biblical faith. As far as the Renaissance is concerned it is doubtful whether any Renaissance figures would be congenial to the twentieth century. One must, of course, cast out the beat generation whose simulation of abandon is too contrived to be convincing.

Luther, that figure most associated with the crash of the Catholic world, is perhaps one of the most appreciated and the least understood of all medieval figures. He has probably been most misunderstood by Catholics who have made him into an obscene symbol and by Lutherans who have made him into an institutional fetish.

But Luther cannot be appreciated by those who enjoy listing his vices or by those who identify themselves with his virtues. The Catholic image of Luther is rarely either fair or the product of disciplined reflection. The Protestant view of Luther is usually pretentious and misinformed.

Luther's contributions of Protestant piety have been catalogued so frequently that a repetition at this point is not necessary since any standard work can be consulted.[24] What has rarely been communicated, in view of Protestantism's hesitancy to discover its own critical principles, is Luther's contribution to the creativity of the skeptical method.

Luther cannot be understood unless one accept the fact that he lived on a level radically different from that of the analytical reason. He did not substitute a Lutheran logic for a Thomistic logic. His radical emphasis on grace, his refusal to systematize, mark him as a strangely Dionysian figure.

Luther was not a primitive; and, therefore, like a poet

---

[24] One of the most illuminating is surely Roland H. Bainton's *Here I Stand: A Life of Martin Luther* (Nashville, Tenn.: Abingdon Press, 1950).

(if one can still be theological and poetic) his principle of vitality was expressed through his understanding of the structure of the biblical Idea. Luther was existentially involved with the Bible: he was not its analyst. It is not surprising therefore that his poetry, in the form of hymns, his culture-creating translation of the Bible into German marked him as a figure more involved with the elusive truth of words than with the hard and fast truths of logic.

Like Jesus, Luther was an aphoristic thinker. Who else could have contributed such audacious and memorable phrases as *Sin bravely, Reason is a whore,* and *Here I stand, I can do no other, God help me.*[25]

Whoever doubts Luther's art should first read Luther—the essay on Christian Liberty, for instance—*aloud* and then attempt to do the same with St. Thomas. St. Thomas achieved a magnificent precision. Luther allowed the ancient prophetic poetry to ruin the virginal precision of logic.

Although few have been able to follow Luther in his pilgrimage, he has left his mark upon both German and Protestant culture. Wherever Luther's piety has been engaged in conversations with general culture, it has made two contributions to intellectual freedom. In the first place, it has raised, long before positivism emerged, healthy questions regarding the singular reliability of analytical thinking. Whatever contribution St. Thomas made regarding the

---

[25] Whether precisely in this form or not is a matter of some historical confusion.

necessity of the mind demonstrating its judgments, it is unlikely that he invested the mind with the keys to heaven. Second, Luther, with his doctrine of man's utter helplessness and his doctrine of the gracious mercy of God, has illuminated the fact that man cannot claim to have invented a relationship and a knowledge which it is only God's right to confer. Luther provides a stumbling block for every Promethean attempt to uncover the divine nakedness. He reminds man that his natural life is emptiness, for only those who are empty can be filled.

Calvin and the Anabaptists provided quite different conceptions. The Anabaptists, on the negative side, tended to be unrestrainedly subjective. Although Luther had Dionysian dimensions, his principle of vitality was within a framework, the written and canonical Bible. The Anabaptists, on the other hand, were truly servants of the Spirit: the Bible was less important. At the same time the Anabaptist vision of a community which lived by the spirit and not by the sword had been an invaluable source for social if not literary and intellectual criticism. The peace churches have provided Christendom with significant opportunities of criticizing the casual and insensitive manner with which ordinary society attempts to solve the problems of justice. In addition to its pacifism the Anabaptist tradition has also helped normal Christianity to recognize that capitalism or any other system of privilege is less than an extension of the kingdom of God. The Anabaptist conscience has alerted the

Western conscience to be critical of easy wars and cruel injustice. That it has done this more sensitively than has either the Lutheran or the Catholic traditions is a steady reminder of the necessary breadth of the Christian faith.

Calvinistic culture has, perhaps more than any other branch of Christendom, been sealed off from the kind of turbulence which the artistic imagination creates. Possessing far too easy a distinction between the saved and the damned, it tended, until the contemporary period, to think in too Manichaen a manner. Although it escaped this easy dualism in at least three areas—politics, education, and the art of making money—Calvinism tended to discriminate too exactly between the covenant people and the world which because of Calvinism's view of double predestination it considered to be expendable.

Certainly Calvin's conception of double predestination represented a grotesque distortion of the biblical insights regarding the divine initiative. Calvin not only forced the art of the biblical narratives to surrender to rigid logic but almost eliminated the possibility of the biblical rhythm ever successfully recovering from the intellectual strait jacket into which he placed it.

However, Calvin, like Thomas Aquinas, possessed the virtues of his vices. If he were unable to utilize the aesthetic to criticize the rational, he was able to make the rational principle do double duty. Thus Calvin's love affair with logic forced him to develop remarkably critical methods for understanding the biblical text. Anticipating modern critical scholarship, Calvin insisted upon clear philological and linguistic principles. In his commentaries, his interpretation usually has been purged of special pleading and almost always involves principles of objective literary analysis.

The Calvinist was never the most sensitive of thinkers but he always attempted to think straight. The culture, not surprisingly, placed an emphasis not upon feeling but upon learning; and, happily, as every student of American civilization knows, Calvinism provided much of the energy to create an educated citizenry. The public schools and many of our universities came into being because the Calvinist believed that a confused mind was even more dreadful than a sinful one. Thus, granting the bias of Calvinistic logic, it was able by ricocheting its interest in that logic to engage in critical conversations with culture.

Modern thought has been significantly cross-fertilized by the creativeness and the prejudices of Lutherans, Calvinists, and Anabaptists. However, the magnificent colors and tones that the modern world has produced have received vitality from other than Protestant versions of Dominicans, Franciscans, and Augustinians.

It is impossible to do more than to mention the contributions of modern socio-political forms and scientific methods. The contemporary Christian, whether Catholic or Protestant, frequently communicates his own intellectual immaturity by the judgments that he makes upon politics. Married either to medieval theories of natural law or to some biblical principle torn out of its context, he views with suspicion "secular" political thinking. It is probable, however, that the secular thinking that takes place in the form of the United Nations is ultimately more sensitive and creative than was that of either the court of Charles V, the Geneva theocracy, or its American counterpart, the Massachusetts Bay Colony. In addition, the contributions of a free science have been far more productive than that of a science either under the control of a papal court or under the control of a judiciary dominated by Bible Belt mentality.

As modernity arose out of the ashes of medievalism it began with a peculiar intellectual handicap: the traditional tools of knowledge had been discredited. Both the Bible and Greek thought had presupposed that the mind of man had some kinship with the reality which it was attempting to understand.[26] Modern man, and not without some justification, could not follow the same road. Therefore, though Protestantism attempted a "return" to the Bible, secular thinkers measured existence without benefit of either the Bible or classical metaphysics. Luther and Calvin were all but affirming that man's likeness to God had been eroded

---

[26] It will be remembered, however, that Hellenism's route was direct, while the Hebrew mind inserted an abyss, a doctrine of Holy Creatorhood and Holy Creaturehood.

by his sin, but modern secular thought cautiously committed itself to the exploration of the world within instead of attempting to determine the relationship of the world-within experience to the world-above experience.

The thinkers who have had most responsibility for shaping the mind of the modern man were neither political, theological, nor scientific thinkers. An Italian historian and a German philosopher have perhaps had most influence upon the intellectual atmosphere of the modern world. The labors of Giambattista Vico and Immanuel Kant have provided the modern world with the confidence to chance a limited optimism regarding its own intellectual powers.

Vico, the father of modern historiography, gathered and gave classical form to the insights of many other critics of medieval and ancient methods of reading historical documents. He developed five principles which have influenced the mind of every modern person who has ever taken a course in history. These errors enabled Vico to compensate for the natural and universal bias present within historical documents: (1) a tendency to magnify wealth, glory, and power of antiquity; (2) the tendency of each nation to exaggerate its virtues and minimize its vices; (3) a tendency for the historian to assume that his subject shares his values; (4) a tendency to assume the integrity of sources; and (5) a tendency to assume that the ancients were, because of their proximity, more knowledgeable than later historians.

[137]

What is so important about this method of thinking is that it applied the principles of criticism to the one area in which medievalism was most vulnerable, its twisted and primitive reading of its own historical development. What St. Thomas did for metaphysics in the elimination of intellectual willfullness Vico did for the reading of history.[27]

The collapse of medievalism meant that the modern man had some hope of escaping from a primitivistic view of history and tradition. The price to be paid required the loss of metaphysical nerve, since Plato's faith in the eternal forms as well as Thomas' demonstration of the existence of God had lost its persuasiveness. Perhaps the philosophers had claimed too much. In any case modern man had to take a more modest breath to see if a new direction could be found.

The beginning of modern philosophy is usually associated with Descartes. It was Descartes who bypassed eternity and grounded modern thought in an exercise of interior logic. *I think, therefore I am* became the point of departure for those who followed. The successors of Descartes, men like Locke and Hume, seemed to be saying that since medievalism had failed to storm heaven, they themselves would not

---

[27] Rome has, unhappily, been far more zealous in insisting upon scientific philosophy than upon applying with equal precision the principles of historical analysis to its own muddy sense for tradition. This is particularly true in regard to its toleration of spurious documents and the insufficiency of evidence regarding its own claims to unique apostolic authority.

climb so high. From Descartes onward philosophy has been more concerned with sense experience, with the order of the mind, and with a kind of philosophical psychology than it has with a transcendent metaphysic.

It was Immanuel Kant, the great eighteenth-century successor to the Cartesian world, who gave modern philosophy its creative direction. By accepting the new limits of thought, by carefully defining the boundaries, he gave modern man the courage to think within a new form.[28] No longer able to ground morality in a transcendental world, Kant "demonstrated" that man possessed an equivalent order for his ethics within the content and shape of experience.

The man who was no longer able to know the noumenal or transcendental world was not thereby lost and helpless. By examining the structure of his thought and will he could find the clues which would enable him to live intelligently and justly. The intuitions of space and time, the categorical imperative of a universal ethical obligation created a new interest on the part of modern man with his own experience. It is unlikely that the contributions of modern sociology and economic analysis could have been made on

[28] Roman Catholicism, unable to demonstrate flexibility in regard to the medieval experiment, has tended to sulk because of its fumble. In retaliation for the decay of medievalism, Roman Catholicism has practically placed the modern world on the Index. It is particularly sad to think that Kant, perhaps the most disciplined and least pretentious of modern thinkers, should be forbidden reading for Catholics.

THE ART OF CHRISTIAN DOUBT

any other basis, certainly not that of the medieval synthesis. Kant, like Vico, had forged the instruments of the modern man's patience.

What have been the contributions of the modern world? None, perhaps, if one measures it from the point of view of the unity of the medieval world. Few listeners, accustomed to the clear musical logic of Bach, can adjust themselves to the atonalism of Schönberg. From the standpoint of those who would like to recreate the terms of the medieval synthesis, the modern world may sound more like a chaotic barnyard than it does a symphony.

It may not be possible, however, to measure one culture so directly by another. Perhaps each culture has its mandate. Medievalism hazarded everything on a synthesis. Protestantism ventured everything on the Hebraic principle,[29] and the Renaissance wagered on the Hellenic vision of the universe. The modern man chose not to gamble. Instead, he decided to peek at a more limited problem. He decided to do what the gamblers had been unable to do, to examine carefully the details of existence.

There is a hidden grandeur to the patience of modern scientists as they attempt to find a principle of order that can emerge only out of disciplined experimentation. There can be no doubt, for instance, that modern sociological

---

[29] Protestantism did not of course sustain its initial explosion. The pathos of Protestantism is that it substituted a dreary doctrinal logic for the Aristotelian logic which it had initially opposed.

theory understands far better than did either the medieval or the Reformation man, the pressure of man's social environment. To be sure, those who look for some overarching philosophy of history will be disappointed. The modern secular thinker does not take giant steps. He has been assigned a less heroic task. By carefully examining the details of human experience he has introduced man to a new critical principle. No knowledge without evidence! No untested assumption, not even in the interest of a higher truth. For this patience Christians are indebted since truth is truth even if the vehicle of that truth is pain.

A contemporary vision of the universe must be composed of many colors. The materials of the past are indispensable. Without a knowledge of classicism, the Bible, the medieval synthesis and the Renaissance and the Reformation, man cannot determine his true lineage. Furthermore, human creativity depends upon a multiplicity of methods. Stimulated by both analytical questions and the a priori of faith the sensitive man is driven further into the mystery of both beauty and order.

There may be some Christians who have misunderstood the complexity of their inheritance: they may prefer some single and more manageable principle. However, the sensitive thinker cannot disregard the exciting diversity of his inheritance.

There will be many, unfortunately, who will engage in special pleading for some single historical formula. However, the modern man is precipitated into a situation in which he cannot easily be provincial. Thrust into the turbulence of diversity, the imaginative and analytical man is forced to select, to synthesize, and to constantly re-examine his structure. His is the opportunity of living painfully but his joy comes from knowing that he has chosen the tension of life rather than the spiritual death of polarized existence.

5 | *Faith and Criticism*

IF THIS ESSAY HAS COMMUNICATED THE ASSUMP-
tion that Christianity has, in actual practice, endorsed the
critical life then the reader has been seriously misled. The
rich fabric of Christendom's thought and life have, it is
true, supplied a vibrant critical coloration. At the same
time Christians have as frequently as not cast their lot
with obscurantism.

Dynamic Christianity's unique insight into the nature of
reality does not exempt Christian institutions from mis-
understanding the laws of that universe to which they claim
commitment. Christianity cannot escape the dread tension

between potentiality and actuality, being and becoming.

It was Kierkegaard, that subtle master of paradox, who first dramatized the fact that Christianity *had to become what it was.* What this strange idea meant was that Christianity had to underwrite its own peculiar destiny. By reason of the divine will Christianity possessed its own *being.* It could never be something other than itself.[1] Christianity stands eternally on the precipice of decision. Should it ignore the world of becoming and live spiritlessly in the world of formal definition? Or should it risk its life in moving from definition to actuality? These are its only choices. It can turn from the world of becoming and live in virginal self-evidence or it can venture everything on existence and live by faith. The byproduct of the first decision is obscurantism; of the second, criticism.

If Christianity is to exist a frontier must be crossed. Life by definition must pass into life by deed. But the frontier can be crossed only at the pass of freedom. Unless conviction risks the precarious it is never transformed into faith.

Unless Christianity renounces the dream world of pure being, unless it becomes incarnate in the world of becoming, it cannot exist. So long as it remains only potential it cannot communicate its message to the real world.

---

[1] It is impossibile for Christianity to be Marxism, Stoicism, or Behaviorism. It can be only good or bad Christianity. It can illuminate the truth or hide it, but it cannot pretend that it is free to be other than what it is.

Only as it descends, only as it embraces all the suffering that existence entails can it fulfill its mission of compassion. And when it ventures forth into existence, when it notes the discrepancy between its theory and its practice then it understands criticism. For then it has lived on the double dimension that criticism requires.

Vegetable life begins painlessly, but human life begins with a scream. Torn into life each child faces an increasing crescendo of pain and chaos. Facing that chaos each person is stimulated to become either a Caesar or a craven. He is challenged either to storm the gates of heaven or to sink ignominiously into inadequacy.

The insecurity of life is *given*. Before it men either master chaos by binding it with an iron order or they flee from it and hide from its terror. But whether they become supermen or whether they hide, insecurity cannot be ignored. It is the basic *given* of all human existence.

In addition to Caesarism and timidity there is a third, and infinitely more delicate, response. Jesus and Socrates faced the chaos of existence with a more fragile instrument, trust. Because of the venture of these two, countless numbers have dared to believe that chaos is the door to the cosmos. On the ultimate meaningfulness of that universe they have placed their confidence.

Both orthodoxy and Pyrrhonism fled from the universe by imposing their fixed and inflexible order upon its chaos: neither listened to the voice and mind on the far side of that chaos. The answers of these dogmatic figures are not accidental. The terrible givenness of life can find the weakness in every man and, finding it, turn him into a Napoleon.

What are the offensive dimensions of existence? Human insecurity arises out of a threefold onslaught of chaos: contemporaneity, ambiguity, and particularity.

CONTEMPORANEITY

Contemporaneity is more than the present. The present is only a matter of chronology. Contemporaneity is the present with teeth: it is the present being rude and ungracious, insisting that it be heard on its own terms. Thus the contemporary is always an affront to the guardians of the past. The wisdom of the past is contained in a formula. The present has no wisdom to rely on: instead it trusts its multiple virility.

The battle between the past and the contemporary is the battle between civilization and barbarianism: one has form and the other vitality. From the point of view of the barbarian the past lacks vitality. From the point of view of the past the present lacks taste.

Jesus, Nietzsche, and Socrates each lacked taste.[2] Each

---

[2] Read Mark 2:15-27. It becomes apparent that manners mean far less to Jesus than compassion. He eats and drinks with the wrong people, the "proletariat" of the land. He does not seem to understand his obligation to share the standards of respectability. Jesus is as much a threat because of his unwillingness to accept the social controls of his day as he was because of his ideas.

was an affront to his world. The conservative guardian of ancient formulae genuinely suffers a traumatic experience from those who force him to examine the raw and explosive issues of contemporaneity.

The conservatives of the twentieth century are offended by contemporaneity. The heirs of Calvin in South Africa and Tennessee, and the machinery of American Roman Catholicism[3] tend to be bitter because the rude chaos of the modern world has emerged. The Catholic church tends to take communism and secularism as a personal insult. Calvinism sometimes takes the disappearance of colonialism and the weakening of white supremacy as an aspersion on the virtue of the universe. Contemporaneity has frightened both groups of conservatives and pressed them into an uncritical defense of a point of view which increasingly lacks imagination and vitality. A defense of the *status quo,* whether of medievalism or sixteenth-century Calvinistic theocracy has little charm for a world which is moving on.

It is unfortunate that there should be such a repugnance, on the part of conservatives, to receive the thrust of the present.[4] The rude and unformed stuff of contemporaneity

---

[3] Catholicism, like Calvinism, has its ups and downs. For a penetrating analysis which reveals both the best and the worst of Catholic criticism the reader is asked to examine the article by Thomas P. Coffey in the September 3, 1959, issue of *The Saturday Review.*

[4] It is equally unfortunate that those engaged with the present should have so little patience and interest in the past. One thinks especially of the Pyrrhonists.

is the condition of man's humanity. Unless he is involved in that contemporaneity he is merely an archivist.

Contemporaneity is not a matter of taste. Contemporaneity, theologically speaking, represents the freedom of God to redesign his past commitments. God is not the prisoner of his past: he is the terrible Lord of the present. A refusal to listen to the contemporary is a refusal to hear God. It is in contemporaneity that God speaks. And when God speaks history does not stand still: it moves in a radically new direction.

If man heeds the contemporary he is pressed to the point in which he is forced to recognize the jagged lines that separate truth from every formula: When he notes this line he has passed from intellectual drudge to creative critic. As he expresses his skepticism for the utter authority of the old formula he gains the courage to hear and follow new directions.

AMBIGUITY

The second dimension of the given is ambiguity. Man may be convinced that truth is one, but he lives in a world of multiplicity.

The church, as it emerged from the dramatic world of the Bible, made a courageous and necessary entrance into the world of logic. The Nicene Creed and the ensuing formal theology attempted to create a marriage between the language of analysis and of drama. Unfortunately, the church, following the line of least resistance,[5] found it easier to relegate its aesthetic insights to its liturgy while it concentrated its main efforts on reducing theology to pure logic. Thus the systems of Aquinas and Calvin were inescapable.[6]

Protestantism tends to shrink from ambiguity as much as Catholicism does from contemporaneity. In part, Protestantism is particularly deficient because of the peculiar attitude toward the Bible. Centering its entire theology upon the Bible, it has failed to develop aesthetic principles which would enable it to do justice to the non-Aristotelian dimensions of the Bible. As a result, it has, particularly in the wake of the Reformation, tended to produce a theology which was unnecessarily formal and orthodox. Orthodox thought failed to create either intellectual maneuverability or artistic insight. As a result humanist critics have easily dismissed religion because of its inability to make a contribution except to those who have surrendered to its terminology. Bertrand Russell has represented such a general attack on the irrelevancy of orthodox theology:

---

[5] The Nicene Creed, with the exception of the word *substance,* communicates a cosmic drama in which a succession of divine actions is described.

[6] It will be kept in mind that the problem of understanding does not require the elimination of logic but the addition of art. Just as logic tends to freeze systems, art introduces a necessary sense of ambiguity.

My own view on religion is that of Lucretius. I regard it as a disease born of fear and as a source of untold misery to the human race. I cannot, however, deny that it has made some contributions to civilization. It helped in early days to fix the calendar, and it caused Egyptian priests to chronicle eclipses with such care that in time they became able to predict them. These two services I am prepared to acknowledge, but I do not know of any others.[7]

Russell, through his undisguised contempt, has revealed that there are at least two kinds of obscurantism. There is the obscurantism of irreligion as well as that of religion. Russell is, himself, guilty of masking reality by reducing its forms to mathematics and logic. Unfortunately much of orthodox thought has been a mirror to exactly the same lack of humility and ambiguity.

Actually, in spite of orthodoxy's imprisonment within its own logic, Protestant scholarship has revealed a capacity for *learning* that transcends that of some of its critics. David Hume, the father of empiricism, was so enamored of his own system that he would not tolerate any philosophy which lived independently of *his* categories. Thus, Hume says,

When we run over libraries, persuaded of these principles, what havoc must we make? If we take in our hand any volume; of divinity or school metaphysics, for instance; let us

---

[7] Bertrand Russell, *Why I Am Not a Christian* (New York: Simon and Schuster, Inc., 1957), p. 24.

ask, *Does it contain any abstract reasoning concerning quantity or number?* No. *Does it contain any experimental reasoning concerning matter of fact and existence?* No. Commit it then to the flames; for it can contain nothing but sophistry and illusion."[8]

From this kind of uncritical self-adulation theology has little to learn.

Scholarly Protestantism, in contrast to Hume and to Russell, has accepted contributions of disciplines which transcend the immediate interest and responsibility of the theological discipline. Thus, critical Protestantism, as well as Catholicism and Judaism, have absorbed many of the contributions of the sciences, both laboratory and theoretical. Furthermore, modern biblical scholarship has freely exploited the principles of Vico and, for some decades his rules have formed the presuppositions of biblical analysis. Indeed, the majority of scholarly books produced in the last sixty years have been primarily objective and scientific. Having accepted the tools of literary and historical criticism, Protestantism has demonstrated that it is committed to the doctrine that truth, objectively examined, must constitute the ground on which faith is to be built.

The problem of modern theological scholarship may well be the reverse of the one suggested by its critics. Having

---

[8] David Hume, *Concerning Human Nature* (LaSalle, Ill.: Open Court Publishing Co., 1927).

appropriated secular tools biblical scholarship has all but surrendered its materials to its method. In the name of the Bible Aristotelian order has triumphed over the world of the spirit. The prophets, the Gospels, all have been classified and organized to the point where it is almost impossible for the modern reader of the Bible to penetrate beyond the scientific apparatus itself. Rarely has a student preparing for the ministry had the time to read both the voluminous critical interpretations *and* the biblical material itself. In this sense contemporary biblical scholarship is identical with the worst sins of secular scholarship.

The Nineteenth Century has left a hedge of critical literature about every great writer of antiquity. By the time a student has bored his way through the treatises, he is old, and he is dull. He cannot taste the honey, for he has exhausted himself in cutting down the tree. Let us climb and sip. Three generations of modern scholars have befogged and begoggled their wits over Aeschylus and Horace. Let us never read the learning of these investigators. Let us be ignorant, nimble, and enthusiastic. Let us never drink of that cup of delusion, critical knowledge. A scholar reads the books of other scholars, lest he shall say something that shows ignorance. Conscience and professional ambition keep him at it. He dare not miss a trick; just as the social climber dare not miss a party. Jaded and surfeited, both scholar and climber accept the servitude. They must know all these dull people, because these dull people are in the game that they are playing. Thus, one result of scholars and scholarship is to interpose a phalanx of inferior minds between the young intelligence and the great wits of the past. Must the novice read those forty pages of Wilamouwitz Mollendorff which cover each dialogue of Plato like the grease on a Strasbourg pate?

Scholarship has taken Cerberus from Hades and set him to guard Apollo's hill. Letters have borrowed from the exact sciences a sort of parade of accuracy forgetting that good literature is always inaccurate. When Christ quotes Isaiah, he quotes inaccurately. When Shakespeare or Voltaire, Scott or Byron, or any great writer uses a bit of the past, he twists and distorts it. You will reply, "Ah, but *they* are not professional scholars—the great writers." This is the very question in hand, namely, the meeting-place between scholarship and literature. Perhaps there is a reason why professional scholars are not great writers. Accurate scholarship means unimaginative scholarship. Accurate scholarship, when it prevails, is the epilogue to literature.[9]

The task of Christian thought today is to create writing which will be more than an epilogue to literature. Anchored either within its own orthodox thought or within its more contemporary scientism, Protestantism has been unable to break through to a creative ambiguity. The result is that its scholarship has become defensive, lacks maneu-

[9] John Jay Chapman: *Lucian, Plato and Greek Morals* (Boston: Houghton Mifflin Co., 1931).

verability, and is unable to appreciate the multiple dimensions of the universe which it seeks to interpret.

Just as the Aristotelian principle enables the thinker to classify either the past or already assembled data, so the dramatic principle enables the thinker to face the ambiguity of the present. It is the artistic principle which opens the door to vitality and richness.

It is not without significance, in a world in which reason and intuition are split, that the modern man will need to turn from theology to poetry and drama if he is to gain an insight into the ambiguity and problematic dimension of all thought. In the modern world it is the poets and dramatists, men like W. H. Auden and Arthur Miller, who are the custodians of man's nakedness and helplessness.

One of the dramatists who has most powerfully substituted dramatic nervousness for Aristotelian poise is Jean Anouilh. Particularly relevant is his dramatization of Euripides' Medea. The play opens with Medea facing the loss of Jason, with whom she shared a wild and turbulent youth. Jason, tiring of Dionysian freedom, seeks the security of a respectable marriage to King Creon's daughter. Jason answers Medea's reference to the dreams that they had shared:

I want the world, the chaos where you led me by the hand —I want it to take shape at last. You are probably right in saying that there is no reason, no light, no resting place, that we always have to search with bloodstained hands, strangle and throw away all that we have torn apart. But I want to stop now and be a man. Maybe behave without illusion, as those we used to despise. Just as my father did and my father's father and all those who accepted before us—and more simply than we—to clear a little piece of ground where a man can stand in this confusion and this night.[10]

Medea asks Jason whether he can imagine a world without her.

I am going to try with all my might. I am not young enough now to suffer. I answer the appalling contradictions, the abysses, the wounds by the simplest gesture man has invented in order to live: I discard them.[11]

In the end Medea, seeing Jason walk away, gathers into her speech all the anguish of authentic human existence:

Jason! Do not leave this way! Turn around! Shout something! Hesitate! Feel some pain! Jason, I beg you, all you need is a single moment of bewilderment or doubt in your eyes to save us all.[12]

Thus is spirit crushed by the security that logic seeks.

Modern theology, especially Protestantism, has been so disengaged from the world of art that it has been unable to accept the principle of ambiguity. Facing the chaos of life

---

[10] Jean Anouilh, *The Modern Theatre,* Eric Bentley, ed. (New York: Doubleday Anchor, 1957), Vol. 5. (Luce and Arthur Klein, trans.)
[11] *Ibid.*
[12] *Ibid.*

it prefers *to clear a little piece of ground where a man can stand in this confusion and this night.* Having answered chaos the theologians would prefer to bypass the abyss with a shockingly impregnable view of the cosmos.

Many sensitive Jews and agnostics have faced the sure pens of orthodox thought and hoped for *a single moment of bewilderment or doubt . . . to save us all.* But when theology has triumphed, when its logic has strangled life's problems, neither bewilderment nor sensitivity remains. Only those who are balanced over the abyss can afford to come out from behind their breastworks of logic and meet in the no man's land of . . . human existence.

Christian theologians have every reason to feel embarrassed because the contemporary drama speaks more powerfully than does the contemporary gospel. In part this is because the Arthur Millers and the Jean Anouilhs serve their divinity more directly than do the Christian theologians. The poet, as Plato suspected, is never the servant of logic. Nowhere is the transrational, the Dionysian, better illustrated than in a contemporary poet's evaluation of the sources of poetry.

From the poet's side, I wish to stress two important psychological phenomena: first, that no poet can ever rationally state beforehand what he is going to write about: second, that no poet can rationally state exactly what he has written and why; in effect, what the conflict is or what the new factor is that solves the conflict, until after completely emerging from the mood that made him write the poem. In the second case he may find it impossible to trace even in outline the history of every emblem that occurs in the poem, and an explanation of the poem in terms of logical reasoning that demands a single recognizable character for every statement made in the face of associative complexities and absurdities that the multiple vision of the poet produces.[13]

Unreason, with its testimony to a world of mystery is a threat to every community which attempts to freeze the order of its insights. The resistance to order, the searching for a meaning beyond rationality has been expressed not only by the prophets of the Old Testament but also by those who have served the god Dionysius.

Dionysius—on the immediate level, the god of the vine and sexual ecstasy; and, on his highest level, the god of poetic unreason—represents the forces within nature which break the boundaries of artificial order. Just as the wind and sexual love unleash powers which subvert rationality and control, so do poetry and the drama reveal the soul-shaking chaos which the reason so artificially masks.

Thus Picasso, the most creative of the contemporary Dionysians, has said that *Art is not the truth but Art is a series of lies by means of which we get at the truth.* Picasso speaks with a disarming frankness which is usually lacking in those who think logically and scientifically. Dionysius,

---

[13] Robert Graves: *Poetic Unreason* (London: Cecil Palmer, Ltd., 1925), p. 5.

like Picasso, knows that all thought is founded on distortion and that therefore, the thinker cannot possess the truth. The Dionysian knows that logic cannot fence in reality, and he who thinks with Dionysius knows that he stands on the precipice of ambiguity. The poetic and Dionysian mind not only understands ambiguity but also the child of ambiguity, sensitivity.

The failure of Protestantism to appropriate the insecurity in which art is grounded is particularly puzzling since the Bible itself represents more of a parallel to the Dionysian abandon (which the Bible calls faith) than it does an equation with Aristotelian logic. Although the spirit to which the Bible bears witness and the spirit to which Dionysius bears witness are not the same they are both transrational. The alleged sensuality of Dionysian religion is largely a dramatization of its interior faith in the God beyond and yet involved in sense. So Jane Harrison very creatively epitomizes the Dionysian religion:

> There are some to whom by natural temperament, the religion of Bromios, son of Semele, is and must always be a dead letter, if not a stumbling block. Food is to such a troublesome necessity, wine a danger or a disgust. They dread all stimulus that comes from without; they would fain break the ties that link them with animals and plants. They do not feel in themselves and are at a loss to imagine for others the sacramental mystery of life and nutrition that is accomplished in us day by day; how in the faintness of fasting the whole

nature of man, spirit as well as body, dies down, he cannot think, he cannot work, he cannot love; how in the breaking of bread, and still more in the drinking of wine, life spiritual as well as physical is renewed, thought is reborn, his equanimity, his magnanimity are restored, reason and morality rule again. But to this sacramentalism of life most of us bear constant, if partly unconscious, witness. We will not eat with the man we hate; it is felt a sacrilege leaving a sickness in body and soul. The first breaking of bread and drinking of wine together is the seal of a new friendship; the last eaten in silence at parting is more than many words.[14]

As the sons of Bromius express their intimacy with the gods within nature so does the biblical religion express the relationship of man with the God who transcends nature.

God and man in the Bible are related to each other with an almost Dionysian intimacy. According to one of the earliest stories man receives his vitality from God when ". . . the Lord God formed man of dust from the ground, and breathed into his nostrils the breath of life. . . .[15] Man's life is God's spirit. Like contemporary methods of artificial resuscitation lips are placed to lips and air, or pneuma, is blown into the lungs. Like the sons of Bromius

[14] Jane Harrison, *Prolegomena to the Study of Greek Religion* (London: Cambridge University Press, 1903), pp. 453-454. It should be pointed out that Miss Harrison, like the Greeks whom she so skillfully interprets, conceives of the gift of Dionysius in terms of subtle harmony and not rude excess.

[15] Genesis 2:7.

man received his life from the One who gives him breath. Not by God's logic but by his breath is the world created. Man comes into being because God's oxygen is linked with his own.

In the Hebraic tradition too the spirit of God acts like a wine in that it possesses man and robs him of his rationality. In the earliest traditions God's presence is therefore associated with music and ecstasy.[16]

Later, after the externals of music and the like are eliminated, the spirit of God becomes the authority for new visions of the future. The independence of the prophets is denied, they fall into the hands of the spirit. Like the sons of Bromius they take from God's hands *the cup of staggering.*[17]

In the New Testament, from the point of view of logic and rational order, the situation worsens. The community of the early Christians is, from the point of view of order, lacking in propriety. Its leader is not ashamed to be defined as *a glutton and a drunkard.*[18] The community which emerges by his authority is bound together by more than a rational constitution.

When the day of Pentecost had come, they were all together in one place. And suddenly a sound came from heaven like

---

16 I Samuel 10:5.
17 Isaiah 51:22.
18 Luke 7:34.

the rush of a mighty wind, and it filled all the house where they were sitting. And there appeared to them tongues as of fire, distributed and resting on each one of them. And they were all filled with the Holy Spirit and began to speak in other tongues. . . . And all were amazed and perplexed, saying to one another, "What does this mean?" But others mocking said, "They are filled with new wine."[19]

The wine of Bacchus and the Spirit of God affect the total personality. Neither Dionysius nor the Creator relates to man except in intimacy and surrender. Both visualize fulfillment in terms not of balance but of involvement. Both cause men to stagger.

By logic man retains *a little piece of ground where a man can stand,* but by Dionysius and God man loses everything.[20] He ceases to be an isolated thinker, untouched and unmastered. Drinking of the spirit he becomes helpless . . . he staggers . . . he falls . . . he loves.

Nowhere is this involvement more dramatically illustrated than in that story which is both the liturgical and the theological center of the New Testament, the story which tells of the unity established between Jesus and his disciples over bread and wine:

---

[19] Acts 2:1-4; 12, 13.

[20] One should add that great art also unhinges the system. Anyone who looks at the brooding power of the paintings of Edward Munch or the mischievous power of Picasso needs to take a deep breath and begin to repair his system.

> And as they were eating, he took
> bread, and blessed, and broke it,
> and gave it to them, and said, "Take:
> this is my body." And he took a cup, and
> when he had given thanks he gave it to
> them, and they all drank of it.[21]

The involvement with the true vine means that man loses his objectivity. Knowledge is no longer objective control. Knowledge is now only gained through spending, through the loss of space between the self and reality. God ceases to be an object, even a holy object: he becomes the One before whom man breathes, hopes, and lives.

If the modern man were not a modern man, if he lived within the biblical world, he would not need to rely upon the secular poets and dramatists, the sons of Euripedes. But he does live in the modern world and since theology tends to orbit into an abstraction the insights of modern Dionysians are essential. The Christian is in the position of needing all the help that he can get. If it should be that in accepting this help he discovers a new tension, this is all to the good, for it will teach him a new humility.

The Christian-Dionysian spirit requires that knowledge be acquired through participation. It requires that man lose his autonomy before he gain his knowledge. And in the process of knowing, in contrast to the mastery of logic, his

---

21 Mark 14:22, 23.

vulnerability and ambiguity increase in direct relation to his knowledge. The higher his knowledge the less his certainty. When man balances what he has learned with the fragility of his conviction he lives in sensitive ambiguity.

Man becomes human in the measure that he is enabled to accept the givenness of life. If he cannot accept the terms of his existence, if he rejects *contemporaneity* and *ambiguity*, he also rejects his humanity. However, if he is to become his true self, he must cross yet a third barrier, particularity.

PARTICULARITY

As a concept, particularity means more than simple individuality. Particularity is stubborn individuality. It is individuality which insists upon its independence, which resists being subsumed under the familiar. Particularity is individuality which insists on being understood from within rather than from without.

Particularity is the wife who resists being treated as a general and average woman. Particularity is the boy who refuses to be classified as a typical male adolescent. Particularity will not allow itself to become systematized. Particularity is that element in experience which can never be mastered by the mind of man.

It is particularity which reminds the philosopher, the theologian, and the historian that the universe never quite surrenders. Particularity is the alien within the universe, reminding each thinker that the universe exists independently of the mind and heart of the observer. By means of particularity a thinker discovers that the world stands over against him, that it can never be compressed within his head.

Perhaps the only sin is the refusal to accept the given. It is the Promethean in man which tempts him to believe that he can climb into a universal heaven by ignoring each particularity that stands in his path. The consequence of sin is the loss of reality. Thus, the professional bachelor is unable to accept a particular woman because she does not conform to his ideal and universal standard.[22] He prefers the woman of his imagination because she is his creature; no act of surrender on his part is required. The woman of the imagination lacks the stubbornness of reality, for she only complements man. But a real woman is dangerously real, for she lives within her own explosive right to existence.

A father sins when he resents his son because the reality of the son does not conform to the standard or the universal. The son may lack urbanity. He is not a general son but an awkward, living son. Into the givenness with which he confronts the father he brings his own stubborn particularity. Before such an onslaught of particularity the

---

[22] Not all bachelors are professionals! Some are bachelors through faith. This is to say that they do not marry because their destiny does not in this life lead them to the one with whom they are meant to marry.

father's courage frequently collapses. He, too, needs all the help that he can get.

The rhythm of the universe is this: knowledge comes to man in the measure in which he is able to accept particularity. If he accepts it, he lives creatively. If he denies it, he lives in a world of empty dreams and colorless generality.

Christianity has no exemption from the weight of this problem. If, as it frequently does, it denies particularity, it loses itself in the unreality of universals. If, however, it fulfills its role, it accepts the pain and the suffering that belongs to those who welcome both the foreign and the strange.

What is Christianity but a portion of the Gentile world which has accepted the authority of an experience that did not arise within the Gentile world? Christianity is, in its ultimate sense, an act of courage by which men have recognized that truth came, not through known universals but through the barbarianism of an alien particularity. Christianity is in essence a community which gracefully acknowledges that learning takes place, that knowledge is achieved as man accepts a world which he neither understands nor controls.

Paganism, unlike Christianity, reflects the self-sufficiency of the Gentile world. It is that world which lives within itself, which will not accept the Hebrew barbarian. Christianity, on the other hand, is the Gentile world which opens itself to and allows itself to be instructed by the alien and the particular.[23]

The Gentile, insofar as he resists the alien particularity, is driven back through his own lineage. Intellectually he is driven into Athens, the homeland of his intellectual and scientific knowledge. Politically he goes back to Rome, the noble experiment which provided the foundations for man's hunger for a universal political order. But the Gentile world is eternally divided between those who accept the particularity of the alien Jew and those who insist on interpreting existence through old and manageable categories.

The acceptance of particularity means that truth comes from a stranger. True religion did not arise out of the vitalities of the ancient philosophies or empires. It was grounded neither in Hellenism nor in Rome. It came through the rhythm of the holy stranger. The stranger was not very distinguished. Neither from Troy nor Mycenae nor Crete nor Athens but from the obscure and little-known foothills of Palestine did the truth come. What the early Gentiles, as distinguished from the pagans, dared to do was to insist that the barbaric names of Jericho, Bethlehem, and Shekhem were ultimately more meaningful than were the

---

[23] Christianity came into being as a self-conscious community as it, in the first three centuries of its history, resisted the temptation to jettison its Hebrew heritage. Although the community soon became, in terms of culture, Gentile, it insisted on reading its history through Abraham and not, for instance, through Augustus and Aurelius.

glories of the ancient and universal cities of the classical world.

To become a Christian a Gentile had to accept an alien world. It was impossible to be a Christian on Gentile terms, for the Gentile was autonomous and complete, the author of his own legitimacy. But if he was to become a Christian, he had to receive that which he could not create by his own intelligence. *To be a Christian then is to be a Jew once removed.* To become a Christian a Gentile must be a a Jew by special dispensation.

Acceptance of the alien raises the question of a double level. Whether he lives in Rome or Washington or Moscow, he must also trace his lineage through Jerusalem. To be a Christian every Jones and Smith must claim Abraham as his grandfather. To believe in the true God, every member of the Daughters of the American Revolution must admit that aliens have been the recipients of wisdom which did not originate with the Anglo-Saxons. To be a Christian is to face the pressure of a disturbing particularity which the mind cannot erase. The pagan lives on one dimension and his mark is his poise, but the Christian is eternally off balance.

It is only possible to be truly human by accepting the particularity of a husband or a wife. One can be a human only by being the father of a particular son. In the same sense, one can be human only by becoming . . . a Jew. But a Gentile cannot be a Jew. He can only receive the Jewish culture which comes to him from beyond.

If a Gentile becomes a Christian without also becoming a Jew, he does not really become a Christian; he merely becomes orthodox and instead of possessing a living faith he becomes a custodian of a set of security symbols.

He who is ashamed to be a Jew is ashamed of the rhythm of the universe. He who allows himself to be segregated from the Jew whether in work or in pleasure remains something less than a human being. It matters not whether it is the contemporary Jew or Paul or a prophet or Moses or Abraham. The Gentile who does not say to the Jew . . . "Teach me" . . . cannot know God.

Christian criticism begins with the loss of parochialism. The Jew is a Jew and, therefore, cannot cross the boundary. He remains eternally innocent. The pagan, however, having hardened his heart against particularity, loses himself in the general. He cannot attain two-dimensional existence, and it is this latter perspective which belongs uniquely to the Christian. The Christian, always both a Jew and a Gentile, is a split-level personality. He lives on the dizzy precipice of Gentile universality and Jewish particularity. In fact he is a Gentile, but by faith he is a Jew.

CONCLUSION

Sensitivity demands that man accept his contemporaneity, his ambiguity, and his particularlity. The task of becoming human—and with this goal there can be no disagreement between religion and irreligion—has as its indispensable ingredient, sensitivity. The irreligious man is no less concerned than is the religious. For the intellectual, man's redemption emerges as man is sensitized to both criticism and wisdom. The indebtedness of piety to both sociology and psychology cannot be measured. The independent thinker has taught man something about the anatomy of his prejudices that the religious man was unable to teach himself.[24] Both Christians and Jews, if they understand the dynamics of their own history, will be grateful to accept truth from *any* available source.

The problem of the modern man is either that he is too humble to create a system or that creating one, he becomes too much its prisoner to have a living relation to the world beyond the system. The difficulty of having a system and being able to move out beyond it is one that threatens every person whether he be a Freudian or a Christian, a Marxian or a democrat. The task of the sensitive thinker today is, then, not to superimpose his philosophy on the world but to use his philosophy as a listening apparatus. To create a position and to be able to enrich that position by moving in and out of it then becomes the sign of the sensitive thinker.

---

[24] The fact that sociologists and psychologists are not usually willing to acknowledge their indebtedness to contributions of the religious imagination means only that religion should not, in the interests of defending its ego, abandon its own commitment to a pluralistic universe.

Indeed, it may well be that the age of the monolithic Christian system is over. It may be that Christianity needs to develop a new form of thinking if it is to communicate with a society in which rigid particularism threatens communication. It may be that it is the task of Christianity to refrain from creating one more closed system and, instead, to undergird and to relate the particularities of art and politics and psychology.[25]

If such should be the task, and surely the world hungers for the modesty which tries to understand, then the religious man will have to find a new image of himself. He will cease to hunger for a philosopher's key that will solve all problems of contradiction. He will cease to covet an abstract harmony and will, instead, following the novelists rather than the rationalists, seek contradiction and embrace it, for it is contradiction that marks the limit of system and the atonalistic relation that the system has with life. The modern man can thus take some comfort from the ancient world, for it was the author of Job who with great sensitivity of heart refused to answer the problem that he had raised.

The Christian will cease to view himself as in any sense

---

[25] It can of course be argued that undergirding and relating itself constitutes a system. Perhaps, but if so it will lack a closed end since the undergirding and relating will not be only of the past but will include the novel and the alien. Hence the system, if it be one, will constantly find itself fractured by its receptivity.

victorious. He will recognize with Picasso that every intellectual must distort if he is to illuminate. The mark of the
Christian man will not be strength but fragility, for he will
have been disarmed by the fact that he is committed to
listening. Christian thought will therefore be characterized
by a quality of fragility and vulnerability. Its breastworks
can easily be stormed, it can lose battles easily and, in its
defeat, receive from the enemy the insights which Christianity could not, out of its own substance, create.

What, one may ask, in view of Christianity's competi-
tive instinct (remember the minorities that have suffered at
the hands of the church), could enable Christianity to adjust itself to the demands of sensitivity? Or what is there,
perhaps long ignored, in its substance which could enable
it to accept its destiny of creative vulnerability?

Or what is the quality of knowledge that Christianity
possesses which distinguishes it from the knowledge of
paganism?

The Christian cannot claim an oak-plank kind of knowledge, for he, if he understands the substance of his faith,
knows that what he knows rests upon a flimsy tissue. Indeed, if he examines that tissue, it soon becomes an even
more uncertain form of intellectual security, a contradiction. This contradiction is centered both in the affirmation
that the Christian is asked to make and in the reality to
which the Christian hopes that he is responding.

The critical dimension of knowledge depends not only

upon a tradition of criticism but also upon the way in which the subject conceives of his relation to reality. Whereas the ancient Platonist conceived of a direct relation between the mind and the real, the modern thinker, following Hume and Kant, conceives of the collapse either of that which was previously considered to be real or the collapse of the relationship. The Platonic theory of knowledge seems to be naïve, and the modern theory of knowledge tends to be nihilistic. Christianity, on the other hand, assumes that man has a relationship to reality which is existent (unlike the Humean) but which is broken (unlike the Platonist). Ultimately, the Christian must claim that criticism depends not only upon knowledge but a knowledge which is fractured: it is the relationship which produces knowledge, and it is the brokenness which produces criticism. Finally, that critical life is sustained by the sensitivity which it creates.

It is in his apprehension of the Messiah that the Christian is thrust deeper and deeper into both criticism and faith. The centering of faith in the God-man, in the union of the cradle and the cosmos, forces the believer to understand that a wise God communicates himself through an incredibly foolish act. The believer, whose understanding is always broken by the paradoxical form of revelation, can never be a knower. So, Paul dramatized the fact that revelation comes in a marriage between foolishness and truth.

". . . we preach Christ crucified, a stumbling block to Jews and folly to Gentiles, but to those who are

called, both Jews and Greeks, Christ the power of
God and the wisdom of God. For the foolishness of
God is wiser than men and the weakness of God is
stronger than men."[26]

The foolishness of a suffering God keeps the believer
anchored firmly within both absurdity and existence. Had
God communicated himself, for instance, either through a
laboratory demonstration or through some system of universal and perfect logic, it would have been easier and
more natural for the Christian to acquire an insufferable
knowledgeability about the ways of God.

The paradoxical union of truth and foolishness enables
the believer to return to a dimension from which he frequently attempts flight, creatureliness. The fact that skepticism remains at least a footnote on faith forces the believer
to accept his finitude even while he is accepting God's revelation. Caught between the tension of faith and doubt, the
natural homeland of truth, he acquires not only truth but a
new sense of the dignity of being human. For the glory of
the Christian conception of revelation is this: its form
determines that man shall receive the truth only in the
measure in which he foregoes the dubious pleasure of
affecting an angelic or supernatural existence.

Denied knowledge, he is given sensitivity. Required to
create a cosmology, he is, at the same time, prohibited from

---

26 I Corinthians 1:23-25.

making his system absolute. Because the scandalous abyss of the God-man is the cornerstone of his insight, he is driven deeper into his creaturehood. As a believer, he is asked to become something lower but infinitely more meaningful than a demonic angel.

Sensitized by the humiliation of memory, he hopes for a less reluctant embrace of the humility of God. And yet, because God became man, man, too, may hope to become . . . man.

> ". . . Christ Jesus, who, though he was in the form of
> God, did not count equality with God a thing to be
> grasped, but emptied himself, taking the form of a
> servant, being born in the likeness of men. And
> being found in human form he humbled himself and
> became obedient unto death, even death on a cross."[27]

The memory of the Inquisition and the Geneva theocracy is both shocking and creative. The knowledge of the Promethean moments of Christianity helps the believer to struggle with his predisposition to build invulnerable systems. The Christian is not, after all, a Freudian fundamentalist.[28] He can recognize the limits of his own struc-

---

[27] Philippians 2:5-8.

[28] One of the most creative cross-fertilizations in the modern world has come from the interaction between Christian and Freudian thought. At the same time, while Christians have read and criticized, they have absorbed many of the profound insights of Freud. Freudians, on the other hand, seem to read very little theology. Or, if they do, they,

tures. He need not make a rigid template out of the anthology of his insights. Because he accepts truth via a contradiction, he may hope to assume a more creaturely role in his relations with those who stand outside of his cosmology.[29]

But the Christian can only assume a more creaturely role if he fails to solve the problem of truth. The marriage of foolishness and wisdom can never become a system. At best, it is merely an insight derived from the center of faith. It is not a formula that will enable him to *fix* the relation between art and logic, doubt and belief. The Christian does not, in Christ, possess the philosopher's key that will enable him to unlock the mystery of the universe.

How, then, is the Christian different? Lacking knowledge, he has acquired, perhaps, only patience. Unlike the

---

like the Christian Scientists, get their knowledge straight from the master. Thus, are many Freudians armed for debate with theology, only with a copy of *The Future of an Illusion*. Christians, however, need not be overcome with pride since many Christians have thought that they have understood Freud just because they read Dr. Spock.

[29] The church has frequently made its faith into a sword and a cudgel with which it has tried to coerce conviction. Thus, did Augustine justify the use of force in conversion. Augustine, in writing to the statesman, Olympius, said, "You are of the opinion that no one should be compelled to follow righteousness: and yet you read that the householder said to his servants, 'Whomsoever ye shall find, compel him to come in.' You also read how he who was at first Saul and afterwards Paul, was compelled by the great violence with which Christ coerced him to know and to embrace the truth."

nihilist and the orthodox thinker, he refuses to be driven into a barren corner of the universe. Unable to build a container for the universe, he still seeks the privilege of looking at as much of the universe as possible. He does not stop looking because his system has failed. When, like Job, he discovers that he cannot answer life, he finds meaning in the fact that he is restricted to less than a supernatural knowledge.

Others, Freudians and academicians, may build their foolproof systems, but the Christian cannot excuse the demands of a higher foolishness. And so he accepts a sensitive vulnerability instead of a triumphant system.

And yet, sensitivity is not easily made actual. The Christian rarely achieves the creative vulnerability to which he has been called. He continues to allow himself to be secured by sensitivity-destroying systems. He hides his doubt, instead of incorporating it in his trust. And, when he senses that his vitality is waning, he is tempted to think that he can escape death through the reorganization of his institutional life.

But the believer need not be hopeless. There are ways of recovering creative fragility. He may, and should, reread the thought of Jesus and the passion of Socrates. He may look to his history and discover that Christianity has always understood that its vitality depends, in part, upon the contributions of the world. Doing so, he will be saved from self-sufficiency. He may begin to suspect that the reliance of theology upon logic not only has taken the bounce out of conceptualization, but has suggested too fixed a form of knowledge. He will struggle to disengage himself from the straight lines of rationalism and to avail himself of the ambiguity and mystery of both art and contemporaneity. He may struggle again, as have the saints before him, with the absurd. But, above all, he will discover that creativity cannot be forced, that there are moments when men must live within a dreadful silence. He may need to discover that God does not create until after his spirit has brooded long over the waters. He will need to discover new reservoirs of patience to accept the fact that God's brooding is not yet over.

But waiting need not culminate in either nihilism or despair. Man can learn to live in the night. And, if a man can accept his helplessness, he has hope. If he refuses to climb out of his humanity, he has recovered something of the iron that enables him to exist.

The Christian knows something of his reluctance to be both critical and sensitive: he calls that reluctance, sin. He also knows that the universe does not allow such reluctance to go unchallenged: he calls the chastening of both insensitivity and obscurantism, grace. He knows that *his* world lives both in sin and by grace. Because he is aware, he cries out:

> I believe that the silence of God,
> the absolute speechlessness of Him,
> is a long, long and awful thing
> that the whole world is lost because of.[30]

and yet he joyfully affirms that "the word became flesh and dwelt among us, full of grace and truth."[31] He who lives, as every Christian must, between profound skepticism and sensitive faith will discover that as his reluctance is chastened, his commitment to critical thinking will be strengthened.

---

[30] Tennessee Williams, *Sweet Bird of Youth* (New York: New Directions, 1959), Act II, Scene III.

[31] John 1:14.

HADDAM HOUSE BOOKS

Beyond This Darkness	Roger L. Shinn
Christian Faith and My Job	Alexander Miller
Primer for Protestants	James Hastings Nichols
Preface to Ethical Living	Robert E. Fitch
The Grand Inquisitor	Fyodor Dostoevsky
Youth Asks About Religion	Jack Finegan
Young Laymen—Young Church	John Oliver Nelson
The Human Venture in Sex, Love, and Marriage	
	Peter A. Bertocci
Science and Christian Faith	Edward LeRoy Long, Jr.
A Gospel for the Social Awakening	Walter Rauschenbusch
The Christian in Politics	Jerry Voorhis
Rediscovering the Bible	Bernhard W. Anderson
Life's Meaning	Henry P. Van Dusen
That All May Be One	James Edward Lesslie Newbigin
The Quest for Christian Unity	Robert S. Bilheimer
The Christian Student and the Church	
	J. Robert Nelson, Editor
The Christian Student and the University	
	J. Robert Nelson, Editor
The Christian Student and the World Struggle	
	J. Robert Nelson, Editor
The Unfolding Drama of the Bible	Bernhard W. Anderson
The Student Prayerbook	
	John Oliver Nelson and Others, Editors

Riverside Poetry

How to Make Friends Abroad   Robert Root

Community of Faith   T. Ralph Morton

Encounter with Revolution   M. Richard Shaull

Politics for Christians   William Muehl

The Paradoxes of Democracy

     Kermit Eby and June Greenlief

The Tragic Vision and the Christian Faith

     Nathan A. Scott, Editor

Conscience on Campus   Waldo Beach

The Prophetic Voice in Modern Fiction

     William R. Mueller

The Renewal of Hope   Howard Clark Kee

Christianity and Communism Today   John C. Bennett

The Christian as a Doctor

     James T. Stephens and Edward LeRoy Long, Jr.

Christianity and the Scientist   Ian G. Barbour

The Art of Christian Doubt   Fred Denbeaux

[181]